BAKUGAN
BATTLE BRAWLERS

D0573534

the masquerade ball

ADAPTED BY Elizabeth Hurchalla
DESIGNED AND LETTERED BY
Tomás Montalvo-Lagos

DEL
REY

Ballantine Books * New York

Bakugan Battle Brawlers: The Masquerade Ball is a work of fiction. Names, characters, places, and incidents are the products of the author's imagination or are used fictitiously. Any resemblance to actual events, locales, or persons, living or dead, is entirely coincidental.

A Del Rey Trade Paperback Original

Published in the United States by Del Rey, an imprint of The Random House Publishing Group, a division of Random House, Inc., New York.

DEL REY is a registered trademark and the Del Rey colophon is a trademark of Random House, Inc.

ISBN 978-0-345-51540-7

Printed in the United States of America

www.delreymanga.com

9 8 7 6 5 4 3 2 1

Adapting editor: Elizabeth Hurchalla
Graphic design and lettering: Tomás Montalvo-Lagos

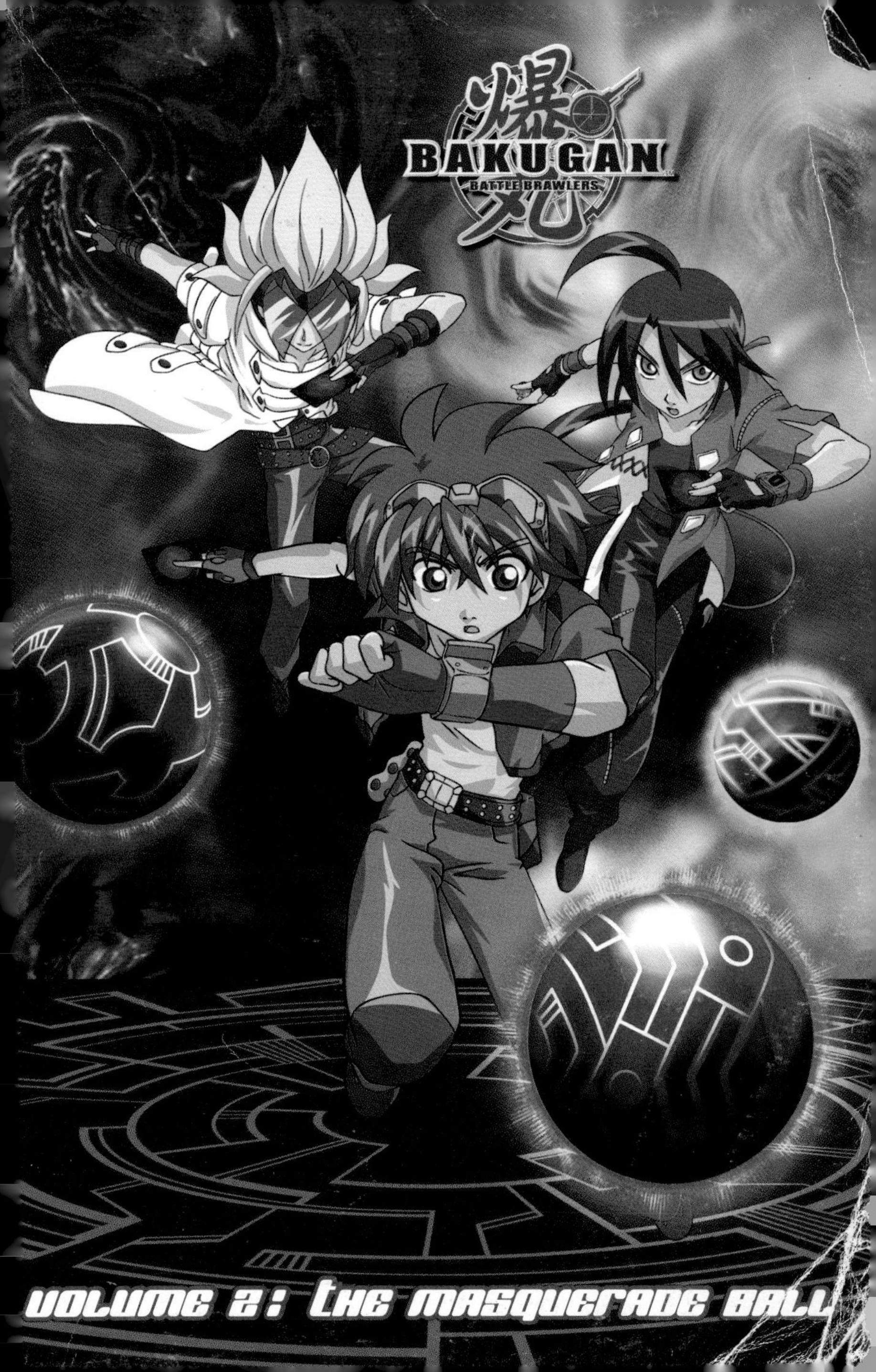
爆丸
BAKUGAN
BATTLE BRAWLERS
VOLUME 2: THE MASQUERADE BALL

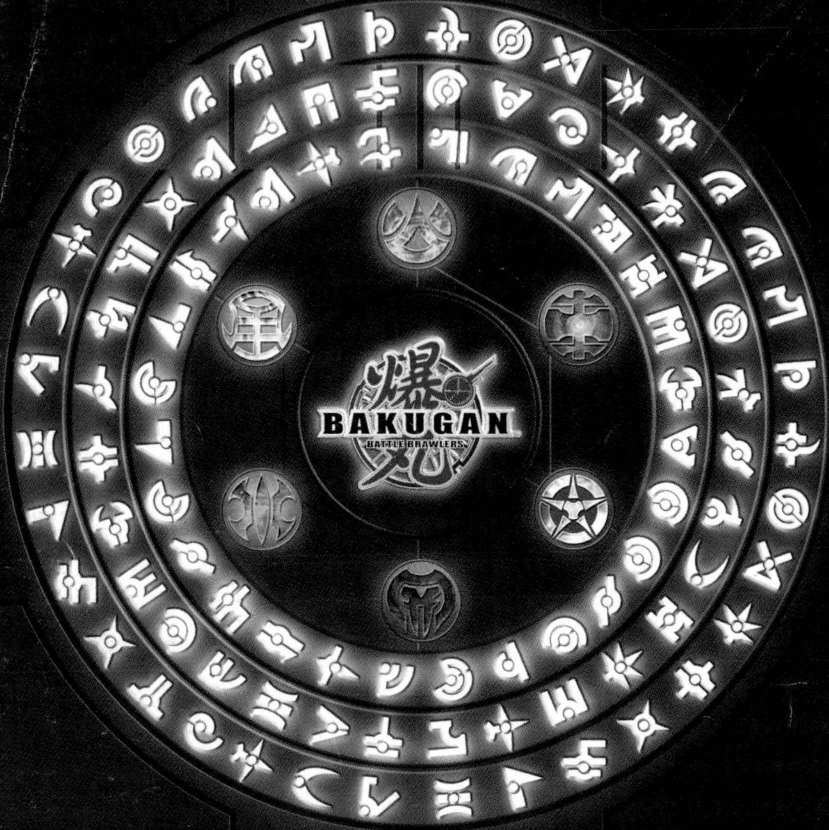
BAKUGAN
BATTLE BRAWLERS

contents

THE CAST OF BAKUGAN BATTLE BRAWLERS™

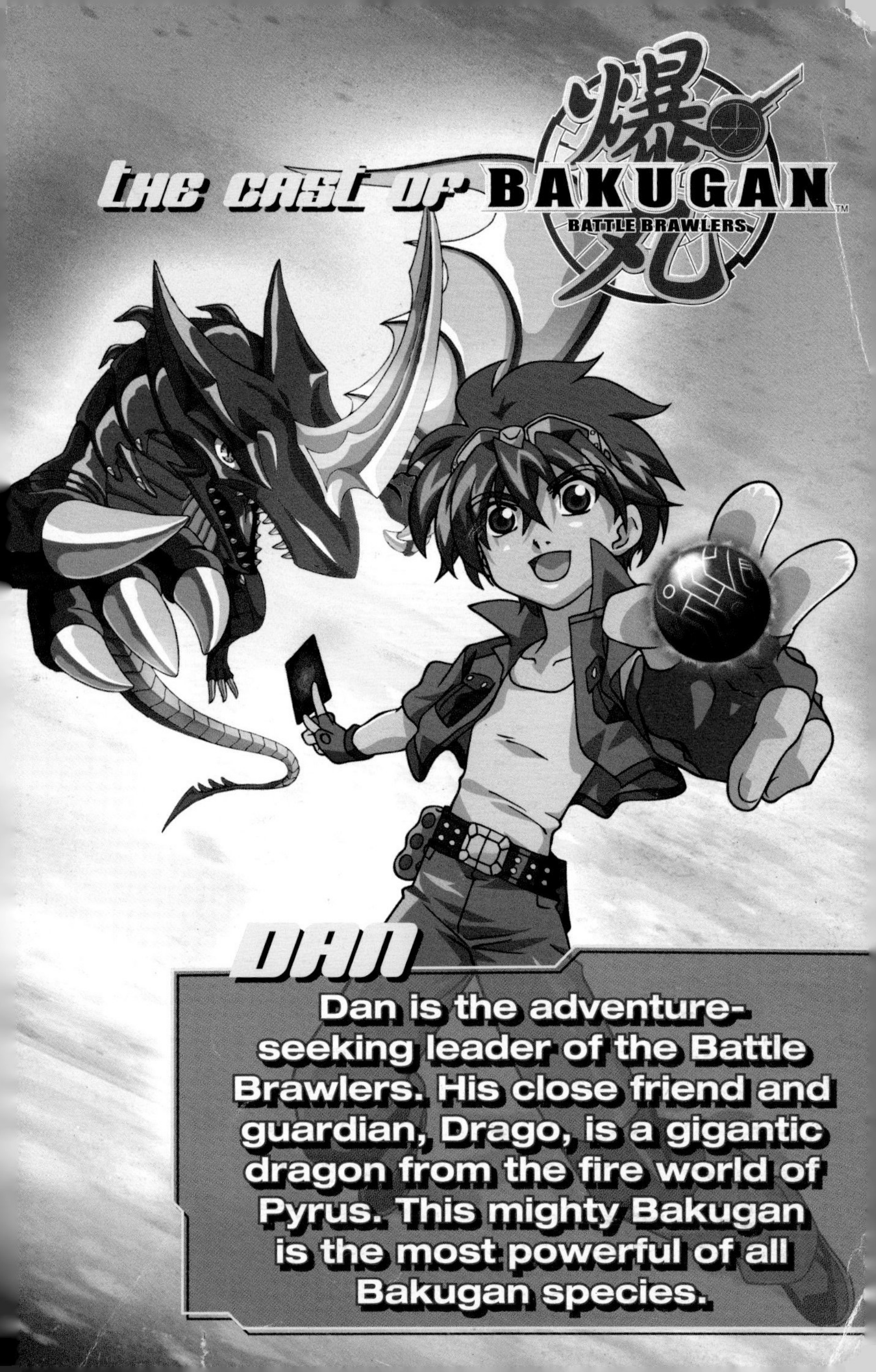

DAN

Dan is the adventure-seeking leader of the Battle Brawlers. His close friend and guardian, Drago, is a gigantic dragon from the fire world of Pyrus. This mighty Bakugan is the most powerful of all Bakugan species.

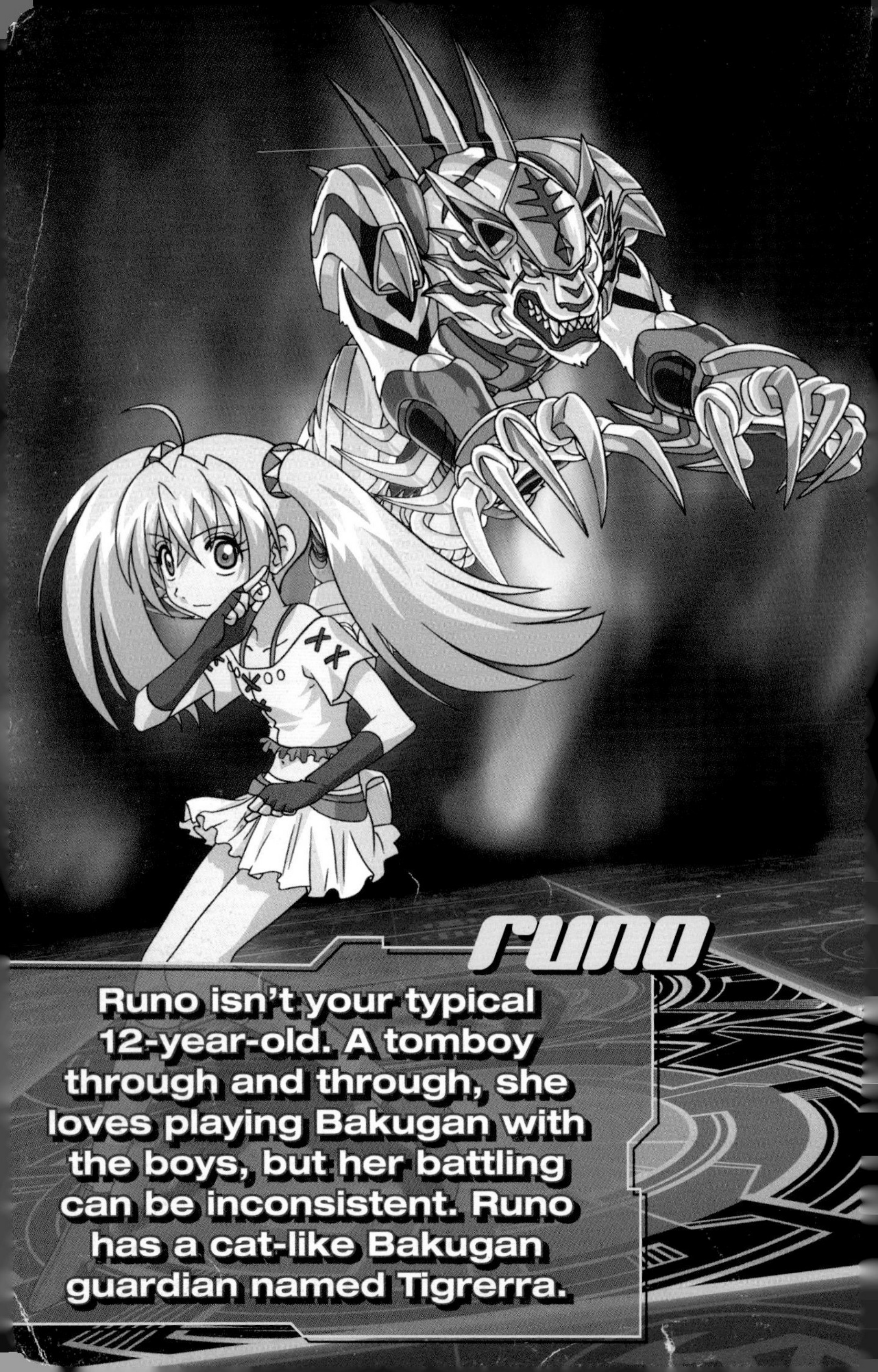

Runo

Runo isn't your typical 12-year-old. A tomboy through and through, she loves playing Bakugan with the boys, but her battling can be inconsistent. Runo has a cat-like Bakugan guardian named Tigrerra.

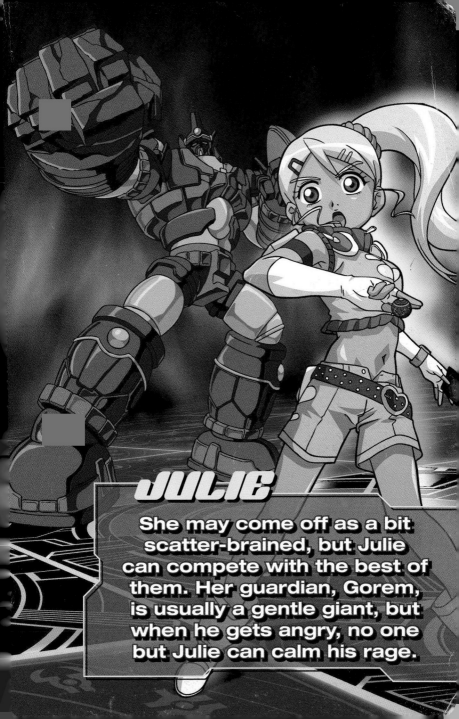

JULIE

She may come off as a bit scatter-brained, but Julie can compete with the best of them. Her guardian, Gorem, is usually a gentle giant, but when he gets angry, no one but Julie can calm his rage.

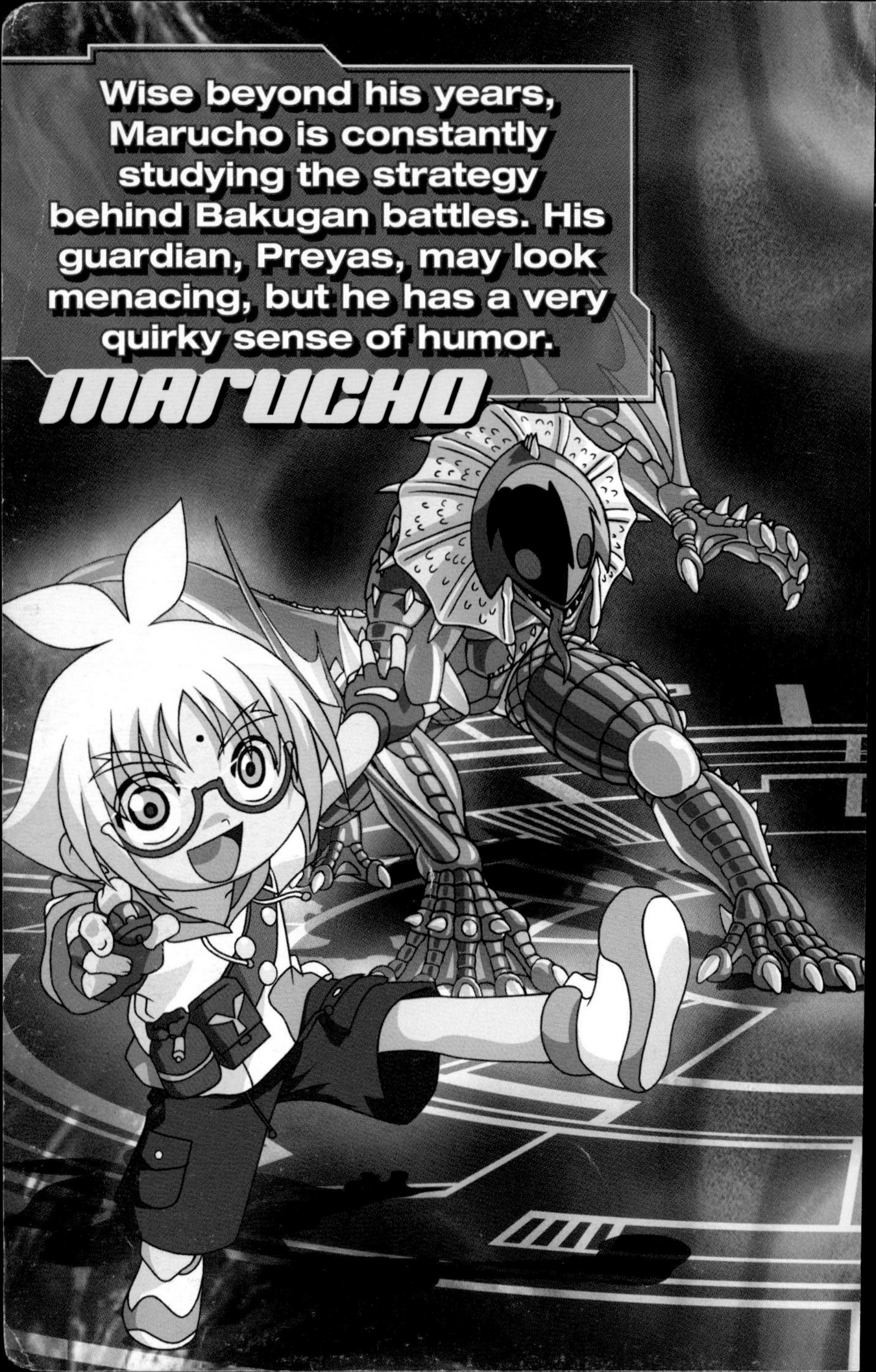
Wise beyond his years, Marucho is constantly studying the strategy behind Bakugan battles. His guardian, Preyas, may look menacing, but he has a very quirky sense of humor.
MARUCHO

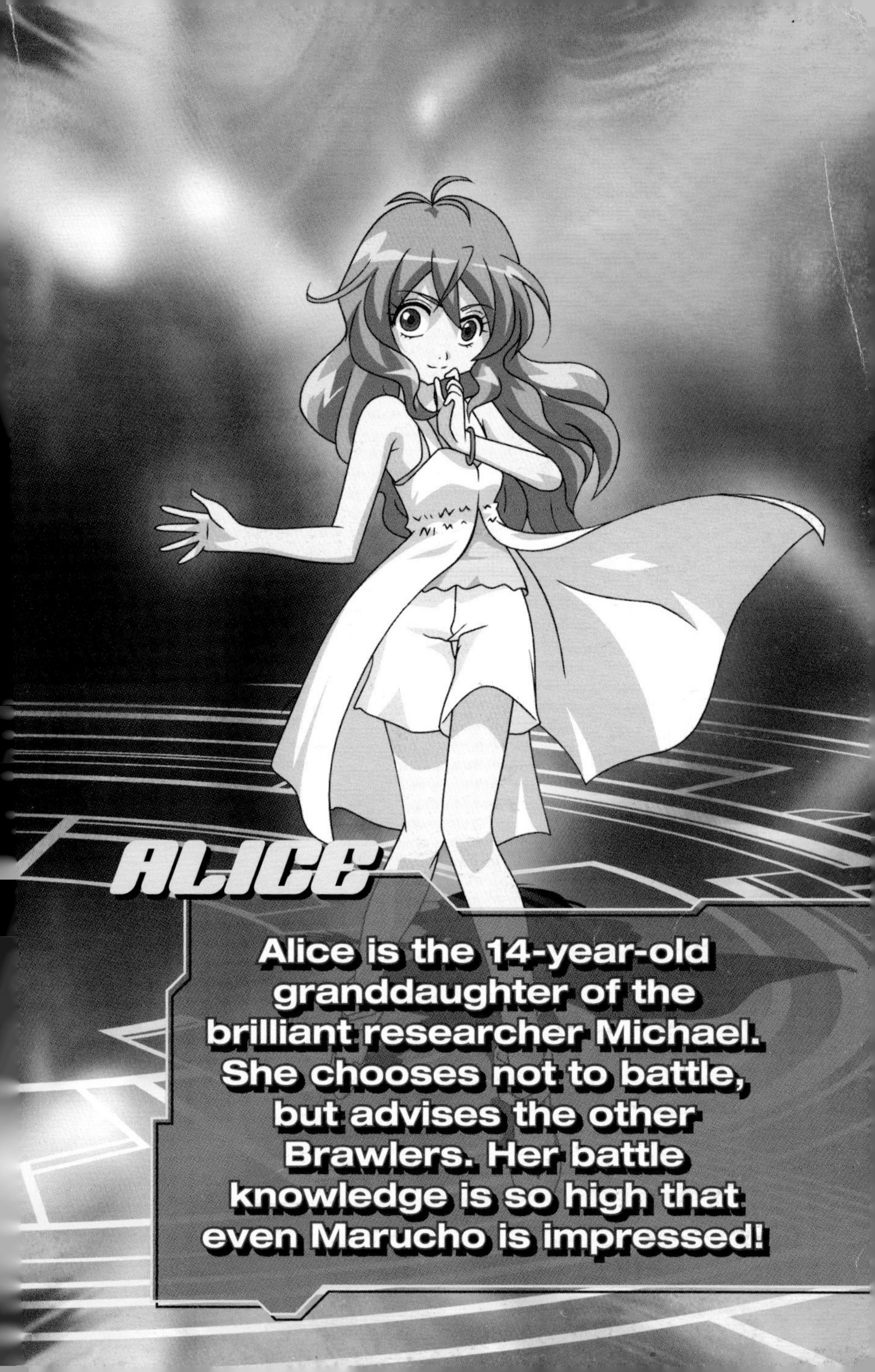

ALICE

Alice is the 14-year-old granddaughter of the brilliant researcher Michael. She chooses not to battle, but advises the other Brawlers. Her battle knowledge is so high that even Marucho is impressed!

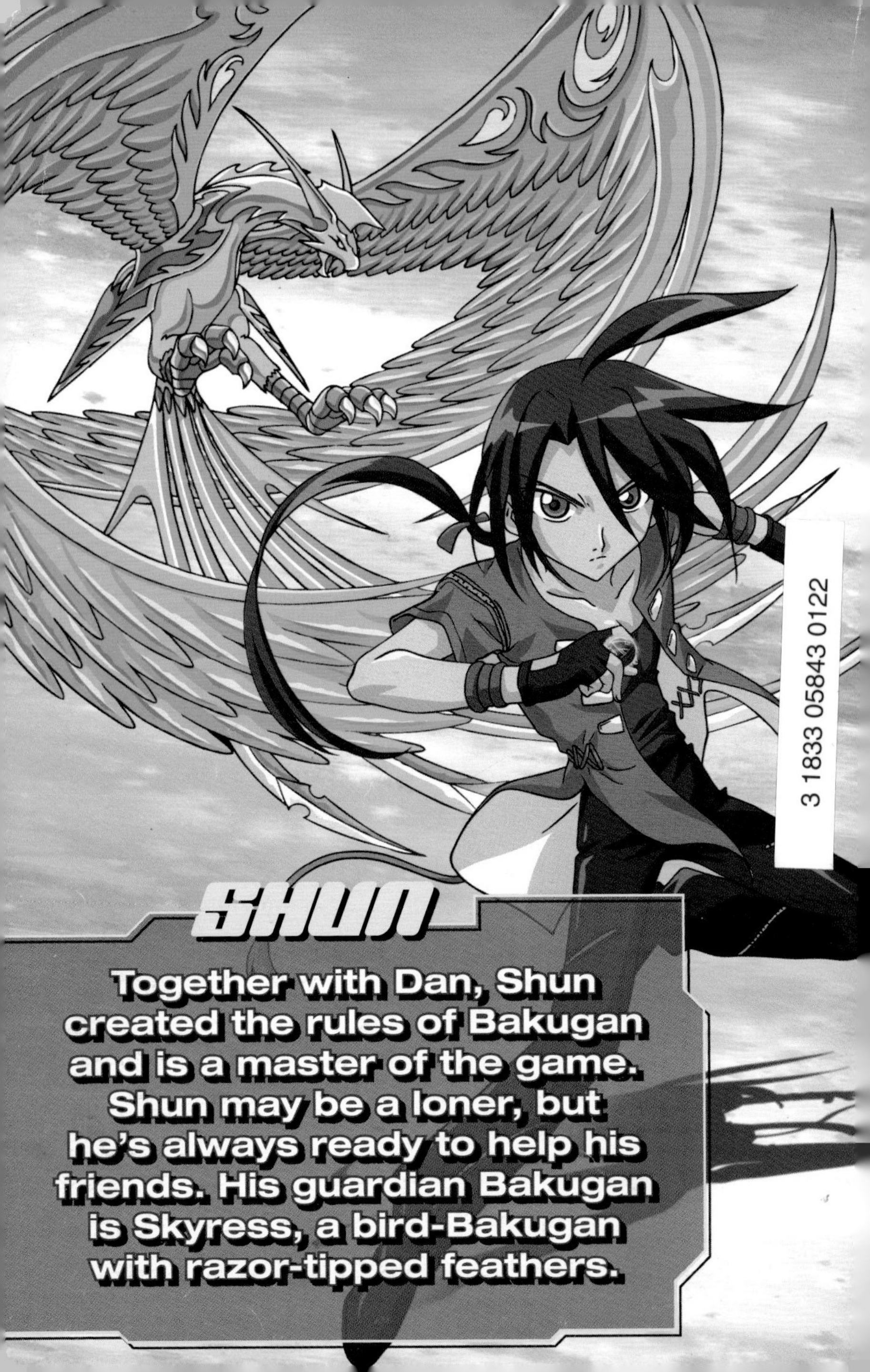
SHUN
Together with Dan, Shun created the rules of Bakugan and is a master of the game. Shun may be a loner, but he's always ready to help his friends. His guardian Bakugan is Skyress, a bird-Bakugan with razor-tipped feathers.

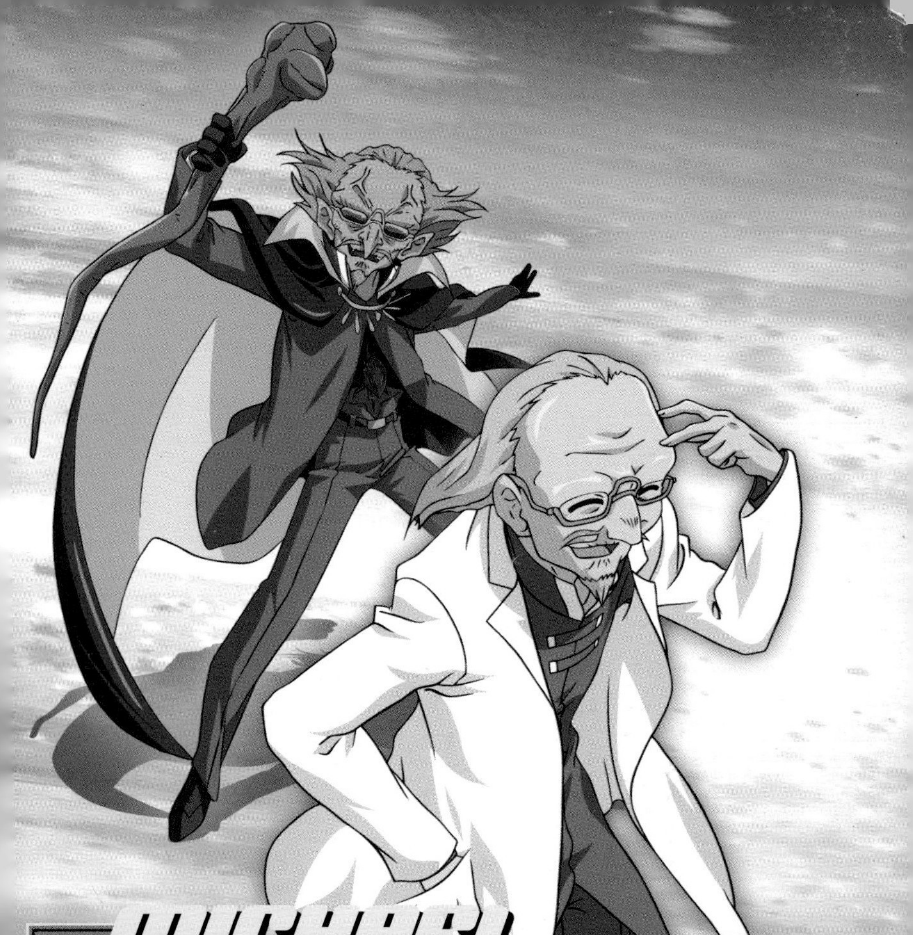

MICHAEL

Michael was the first to discover a portal to Vestroia. After teleporting there, Michael was transformed into the evil Hal-G. Upon returning to Earth, he recruited Masquerade to help him destroy all Bakugan in his way.

My whole world changed one day...

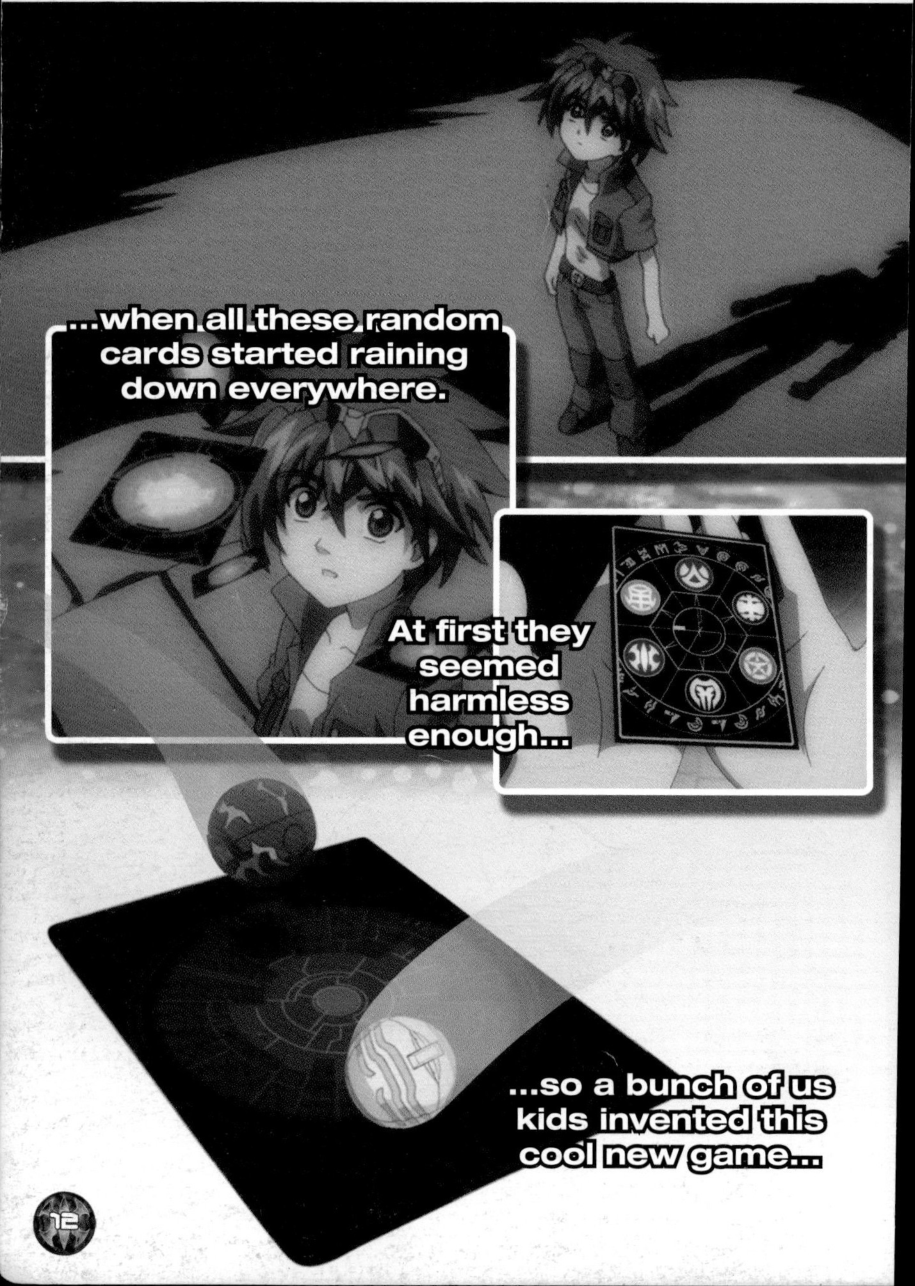
...when all these random cards started raining down everywhere.
At first they seemed harmless enough...
...so a bunch of us kids invented this cool new game...

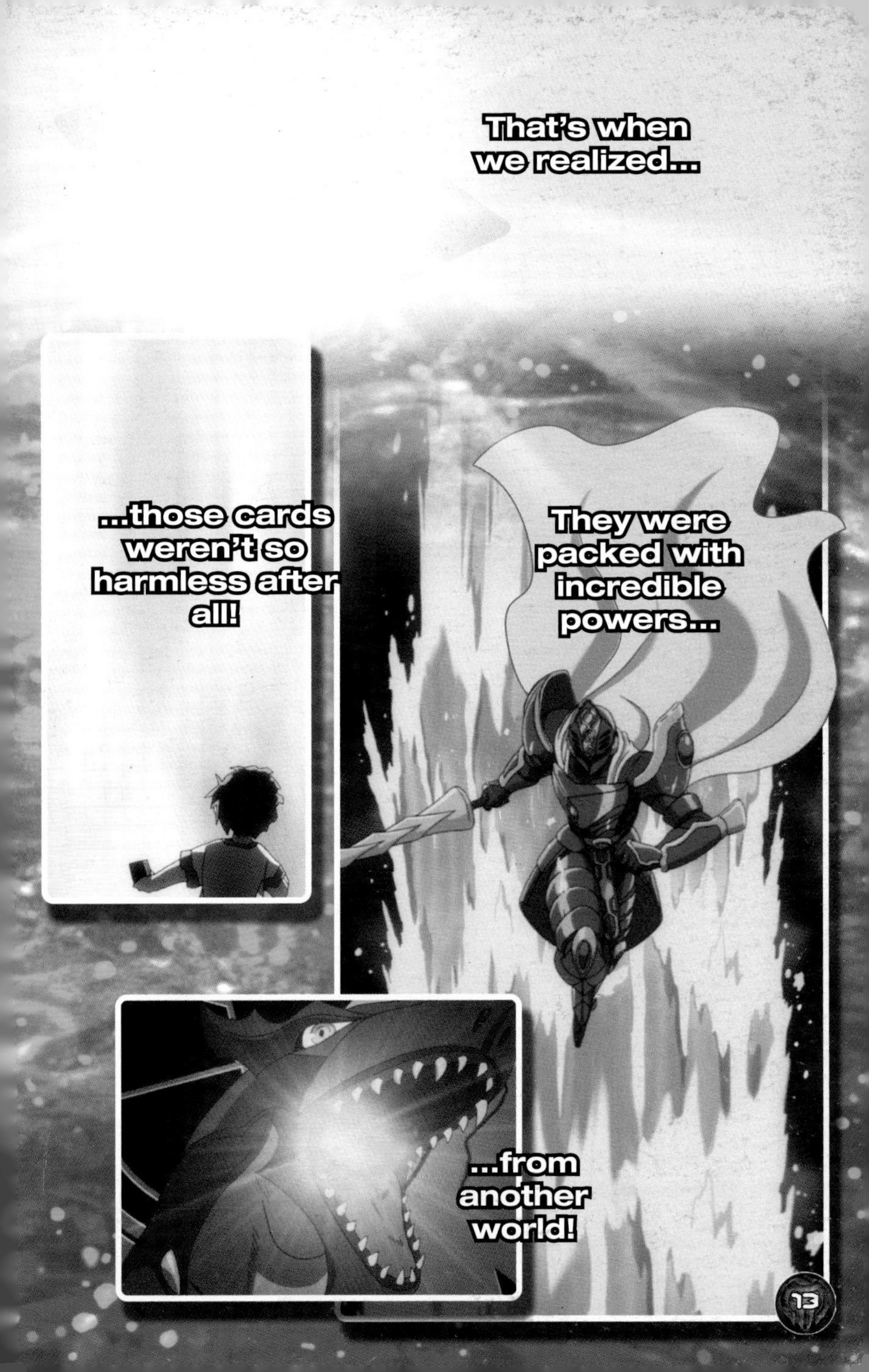
That's when we realized...
...those cards weren't so harmless after all!
They were packed with incredible powers...
...from another world!

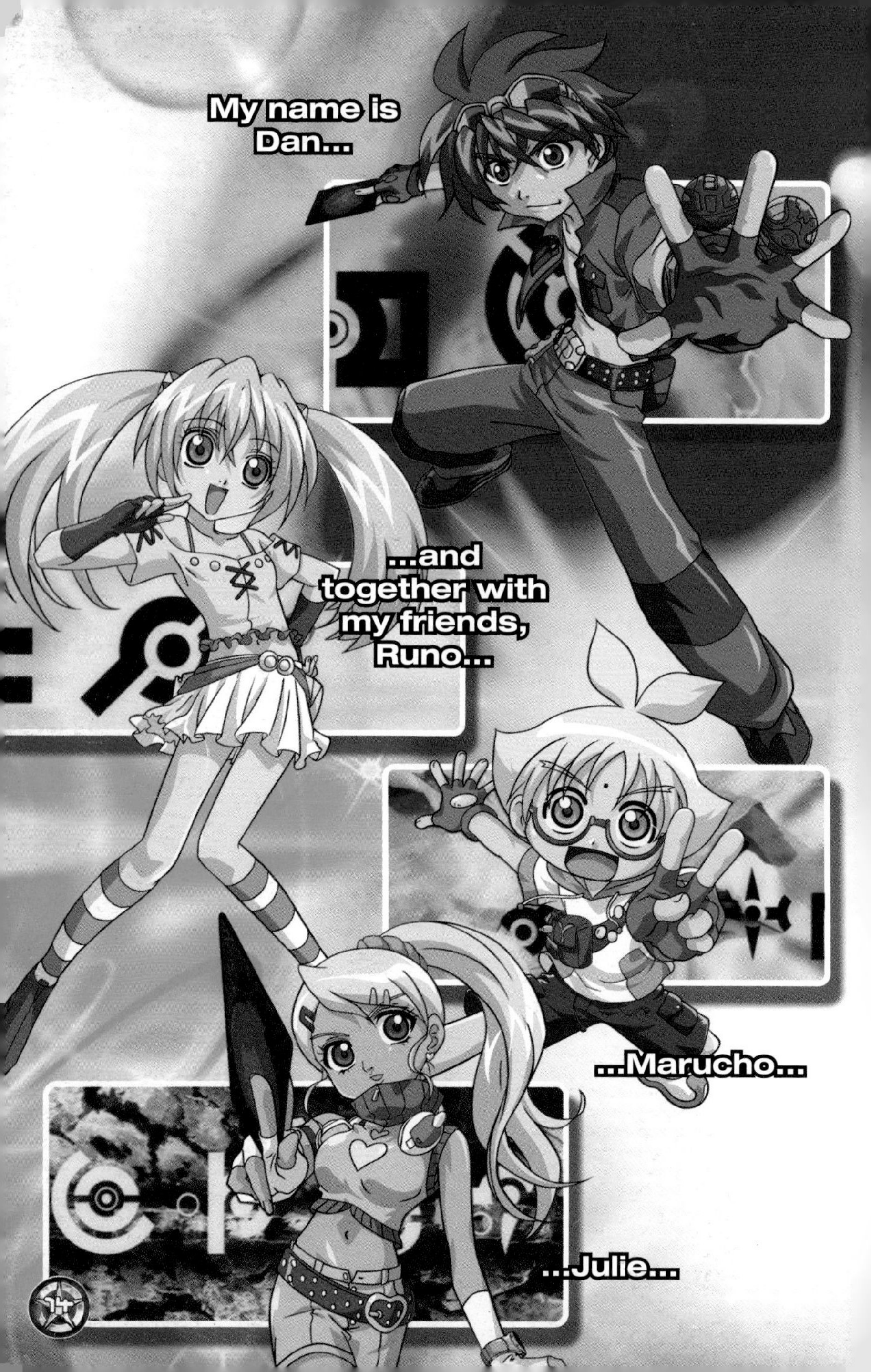
My name is Dan...
...and together with my friends, Runo...
...Marucho...
...Julie...

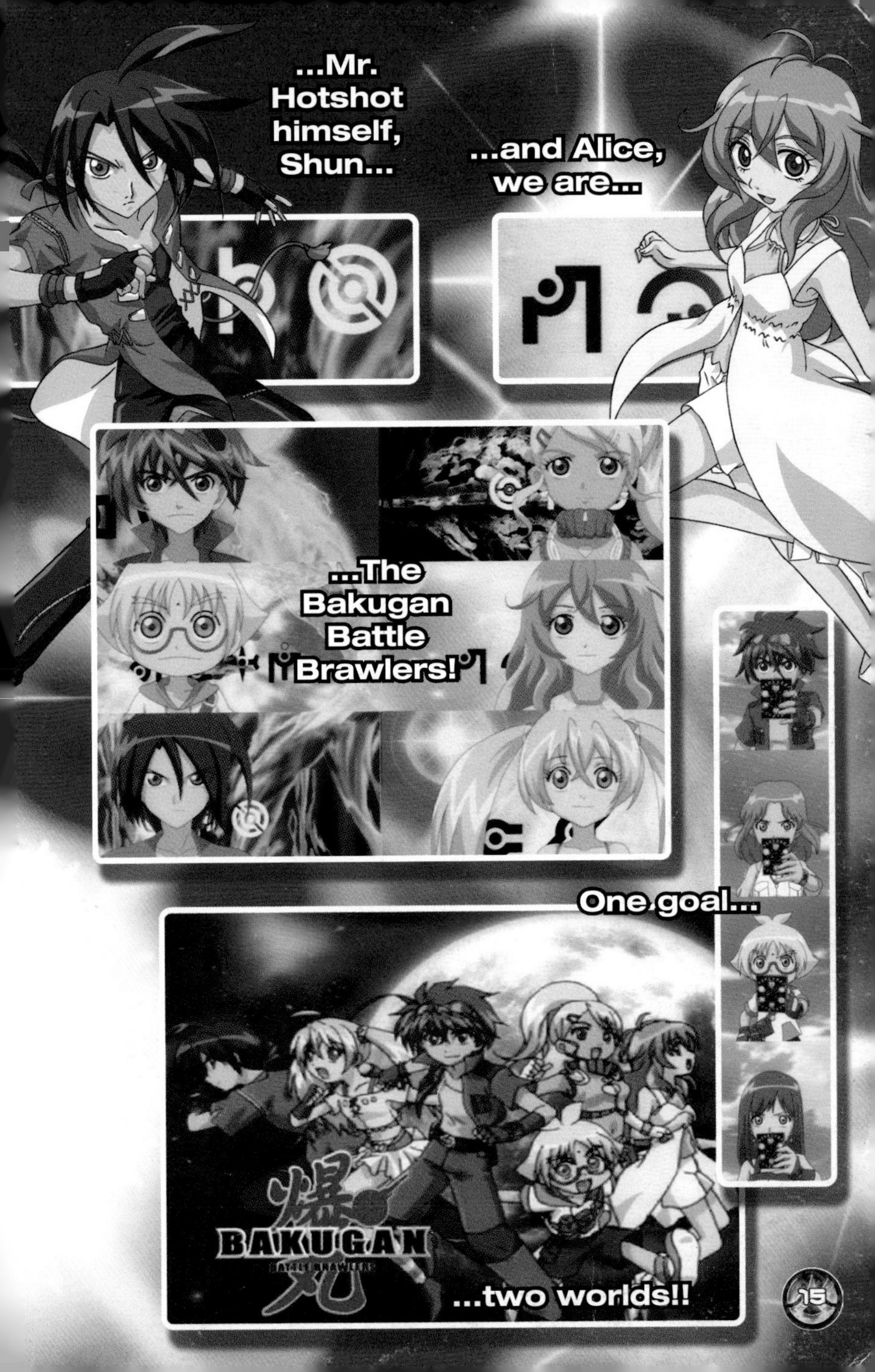
...Mr. Hotshot himself, Shun...
...and Alice, we are...
...The Bakugan Battle Brawlers!
One goal...
BAKUGAN
BATTLE BRAWLERS
...two worlds!!

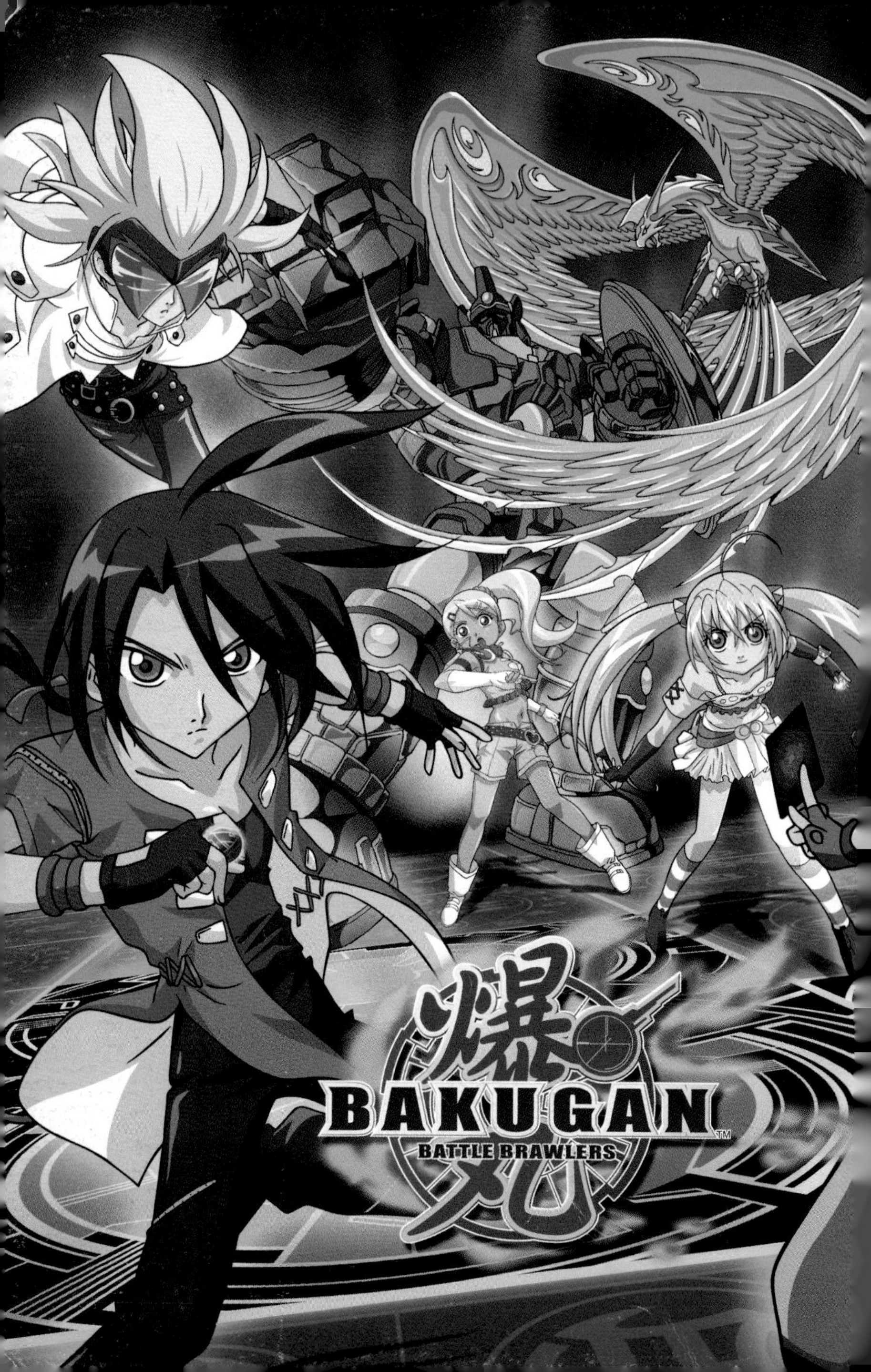
爆丸
BAKUGAN™
BATTLE BRAWLERS

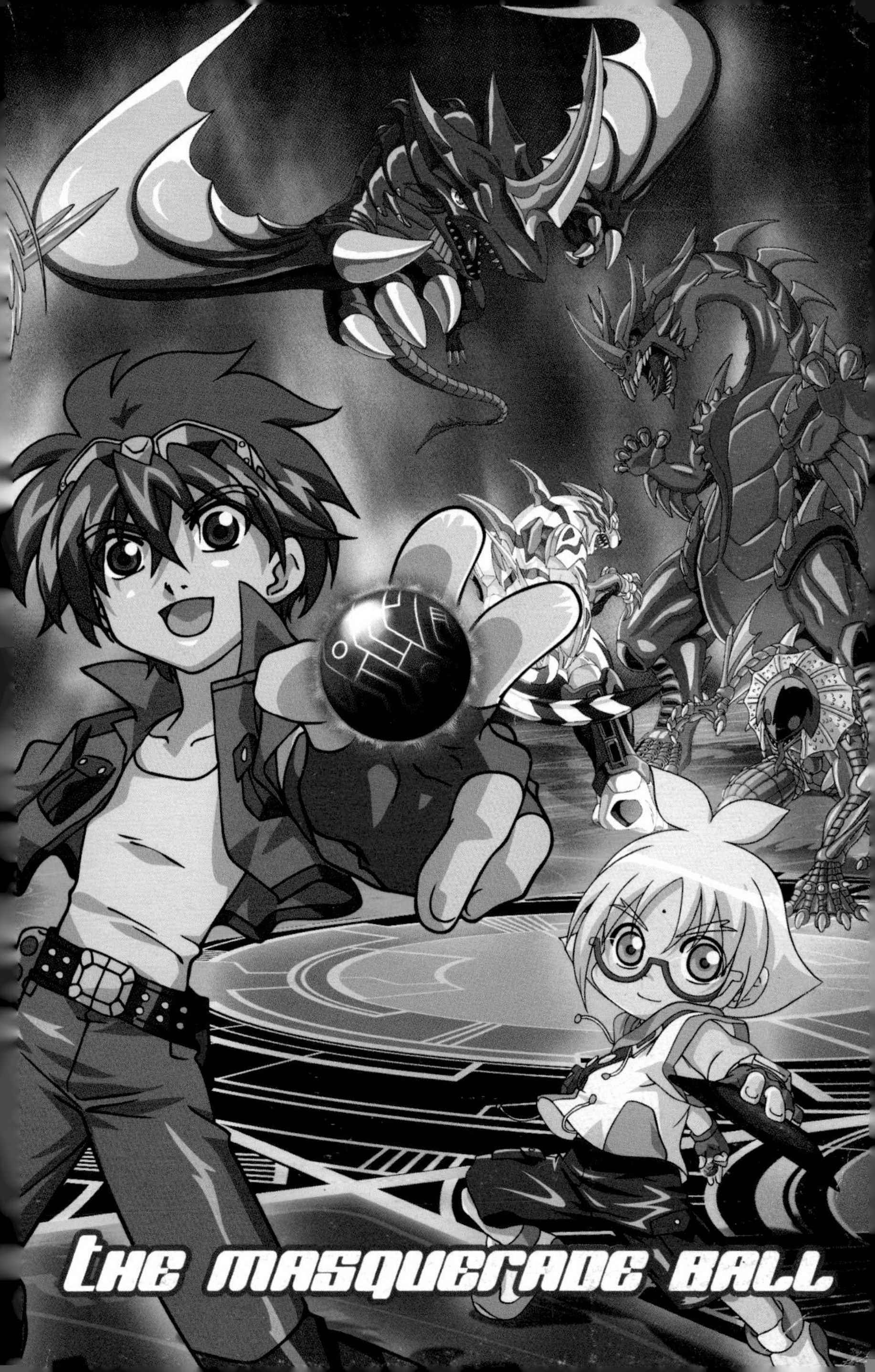
THE MASQUERADE BALL

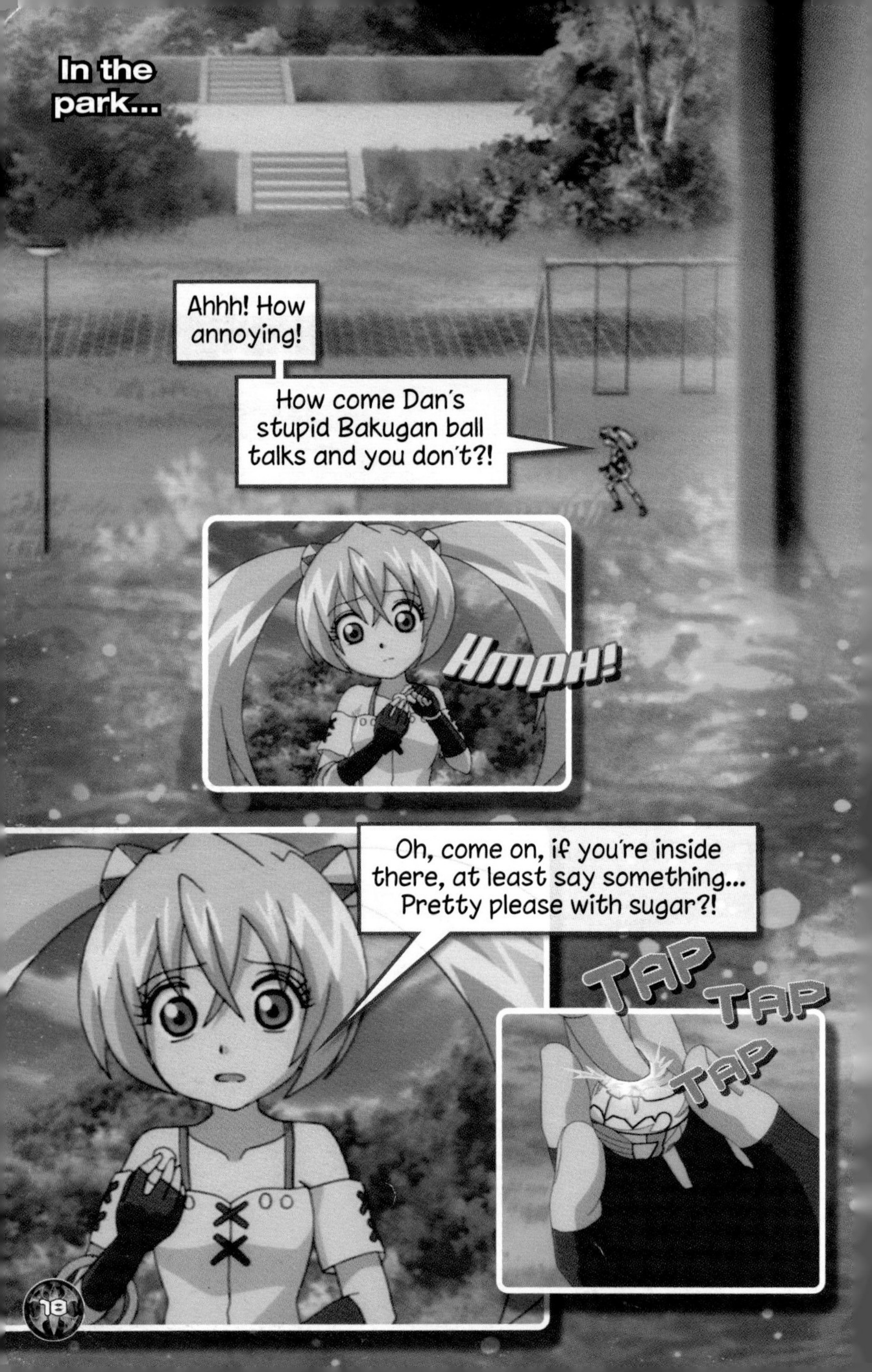
In the park...
Ahhh! How annoying!
How come Dan's stupid Bakugan ball talks and you don't?!
HMPH!
Oh, come on, if you're inside there, at least say something... Pretty please with sugar?!
TAP TAP TAP

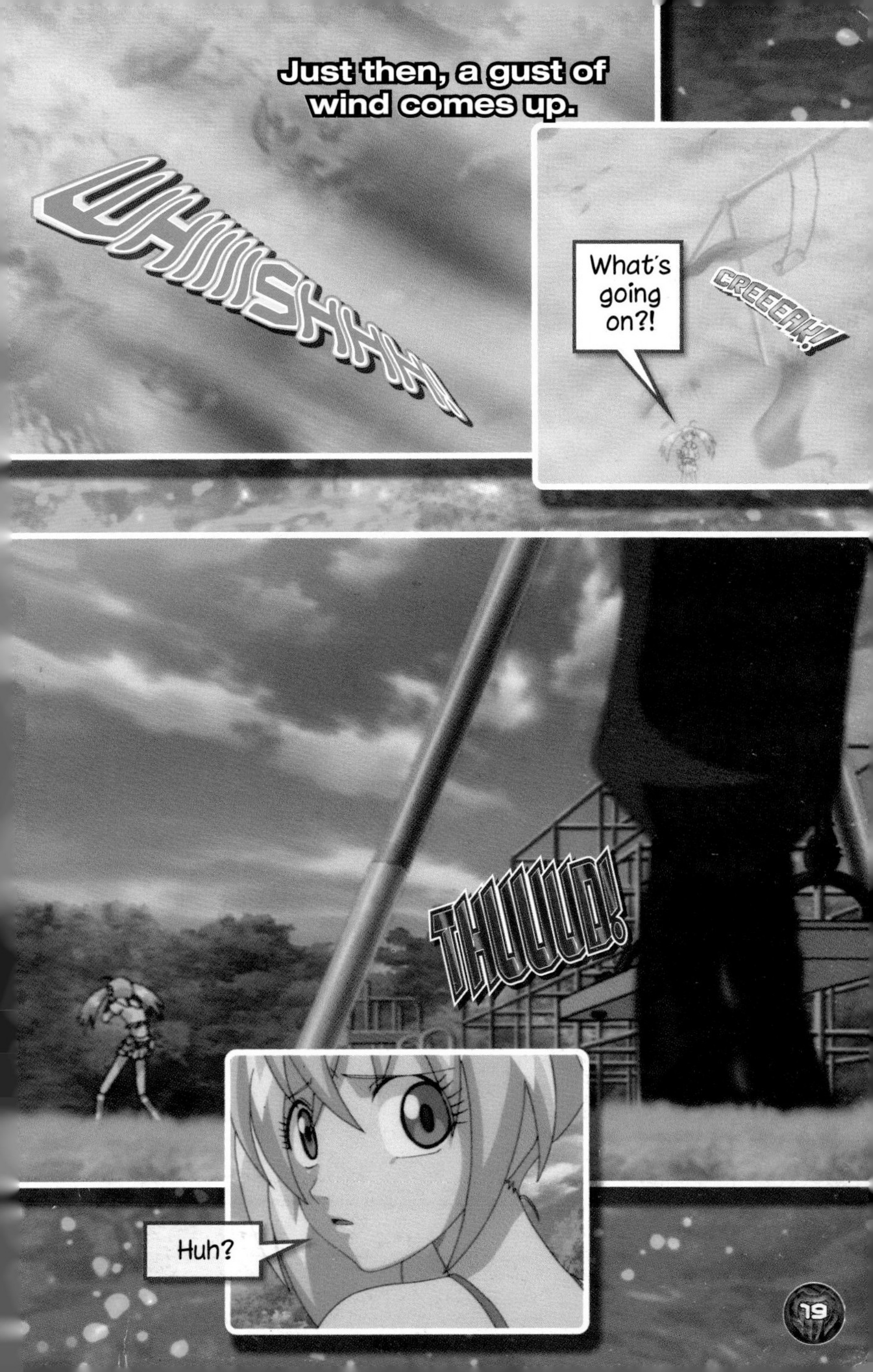
Just then, a gust of wind comes up.
What's going on?!
CREEEAK!
THUUUD!
Huh?

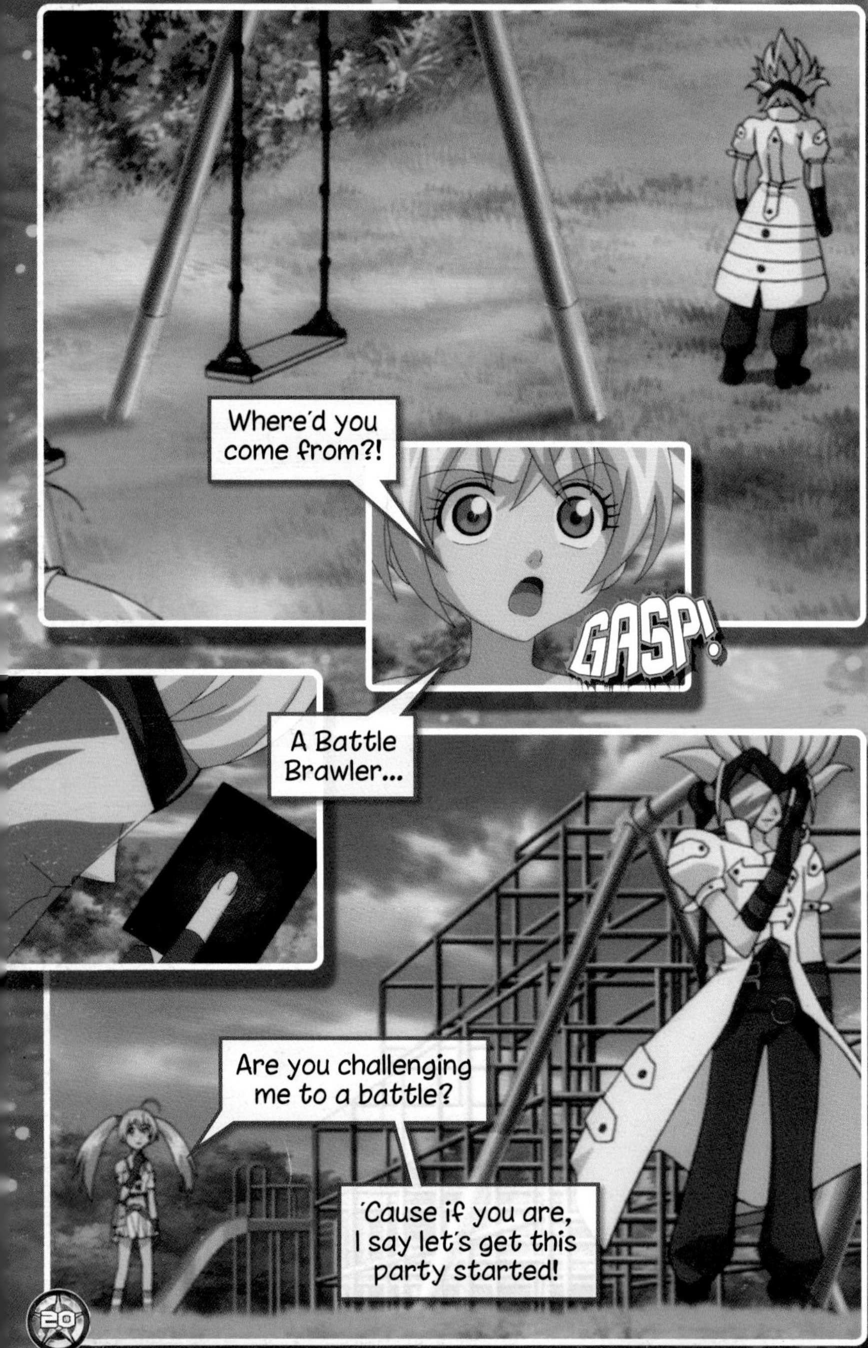
Where'd you come from?!
GASP!
A Battle Brawler...
Are you challenging me to a battle?
'Cause if you are, I say let's get this party started!

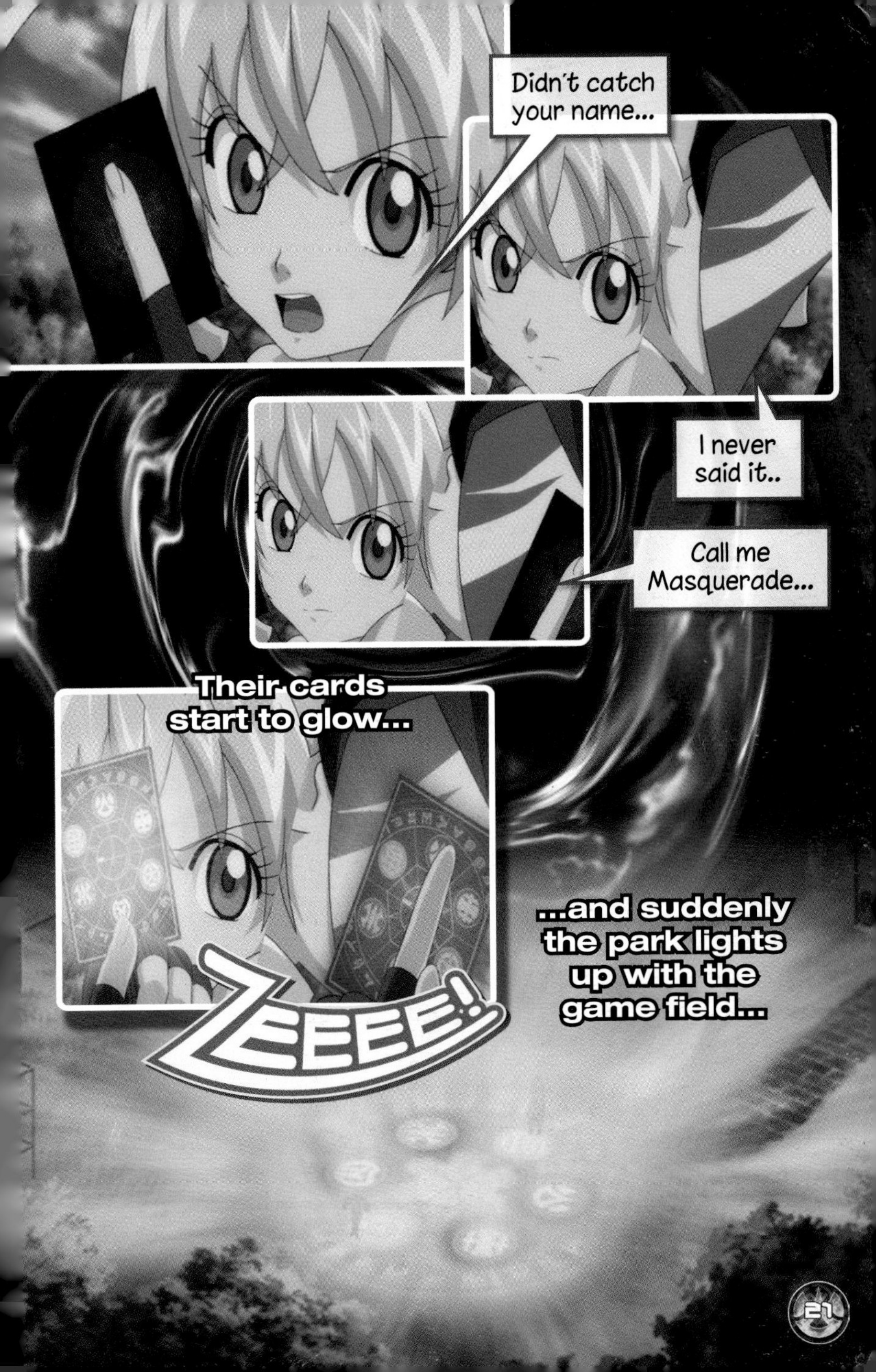

Didn't catch your name...
I never said it..
Call me Masquerade...
Their cards start to glow...
ZEEEE!
...and suddenly the park lights up with the game field...

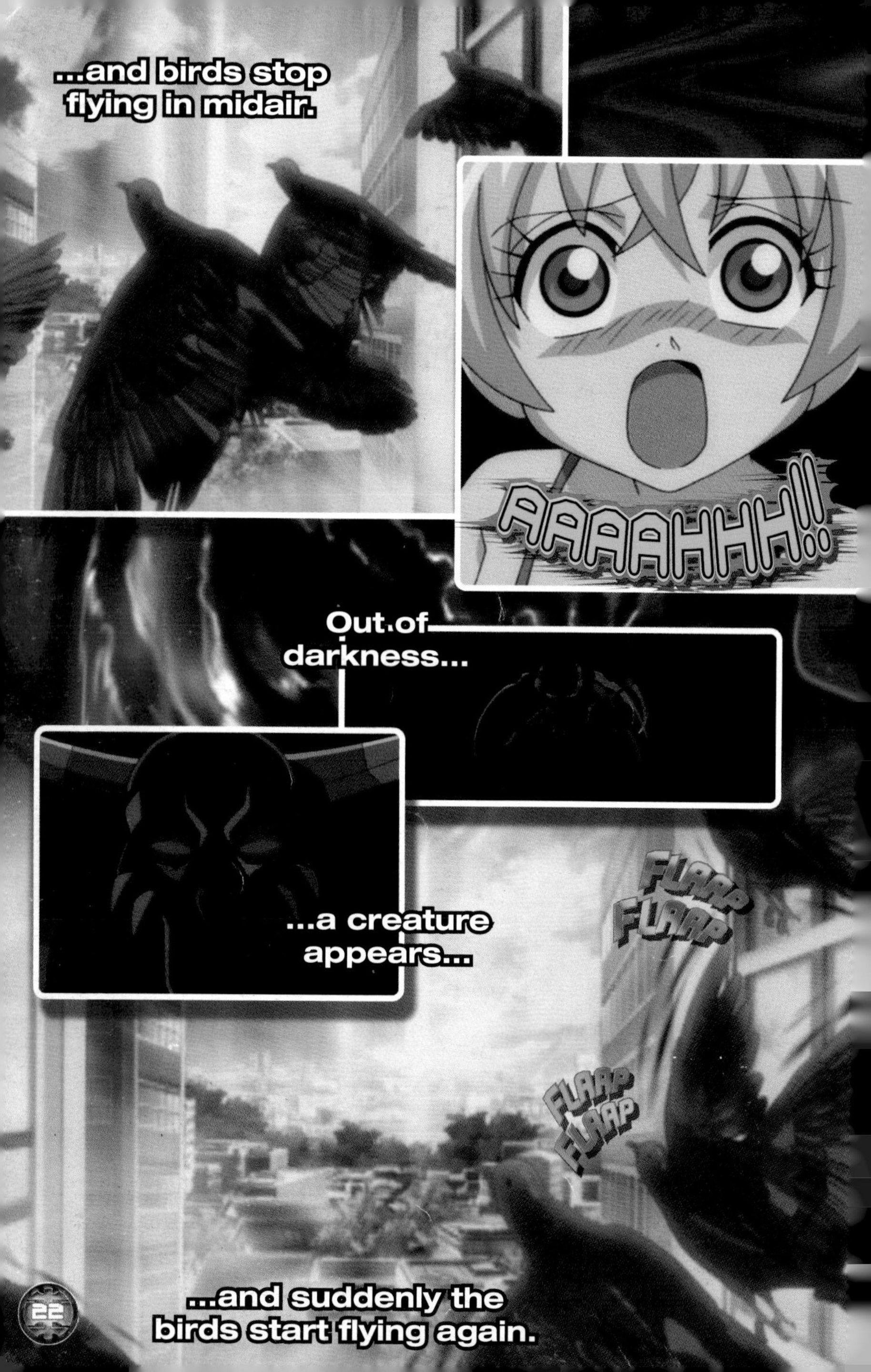
...and birds stop flying in midair.
AAAAHHH!!
Out of darkness...
...a creature appears...
FLAAP FLAAP
FLAAP FLAAP
...and suddenly the birds start flying again.

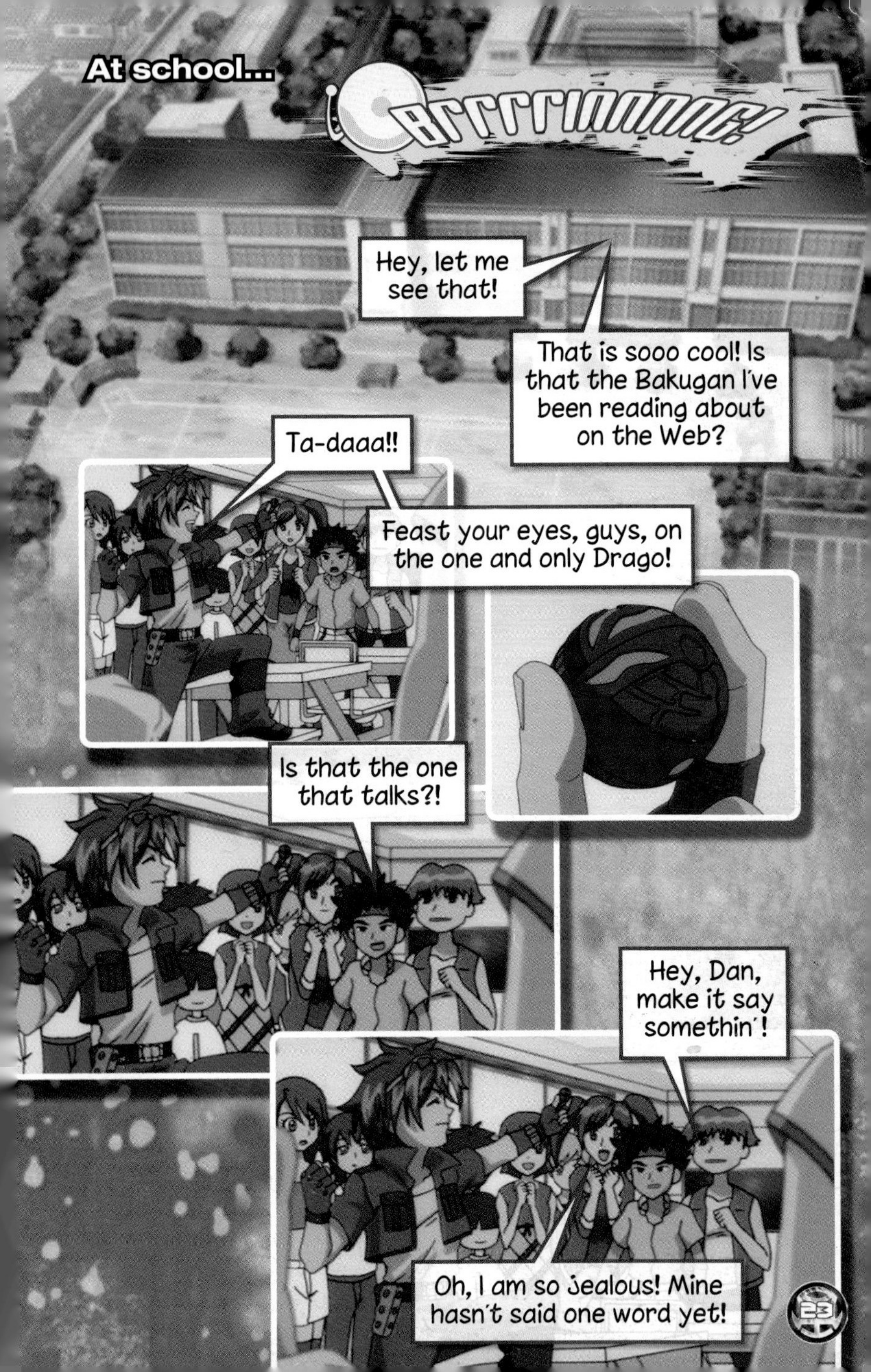
At school...
BRRRRINNNNG!
Hey, let me see that!
That is sooo cool! Is that the Bakugan I've been reading about on the Web?
Ta-daaa!!
Feast your eyes, guys, on the one and only Drago!
Is that the one that talks?!
Hey, Dan, make it say somethin'!
Oh, I am so jealous! Mine hasn't said one word yet!

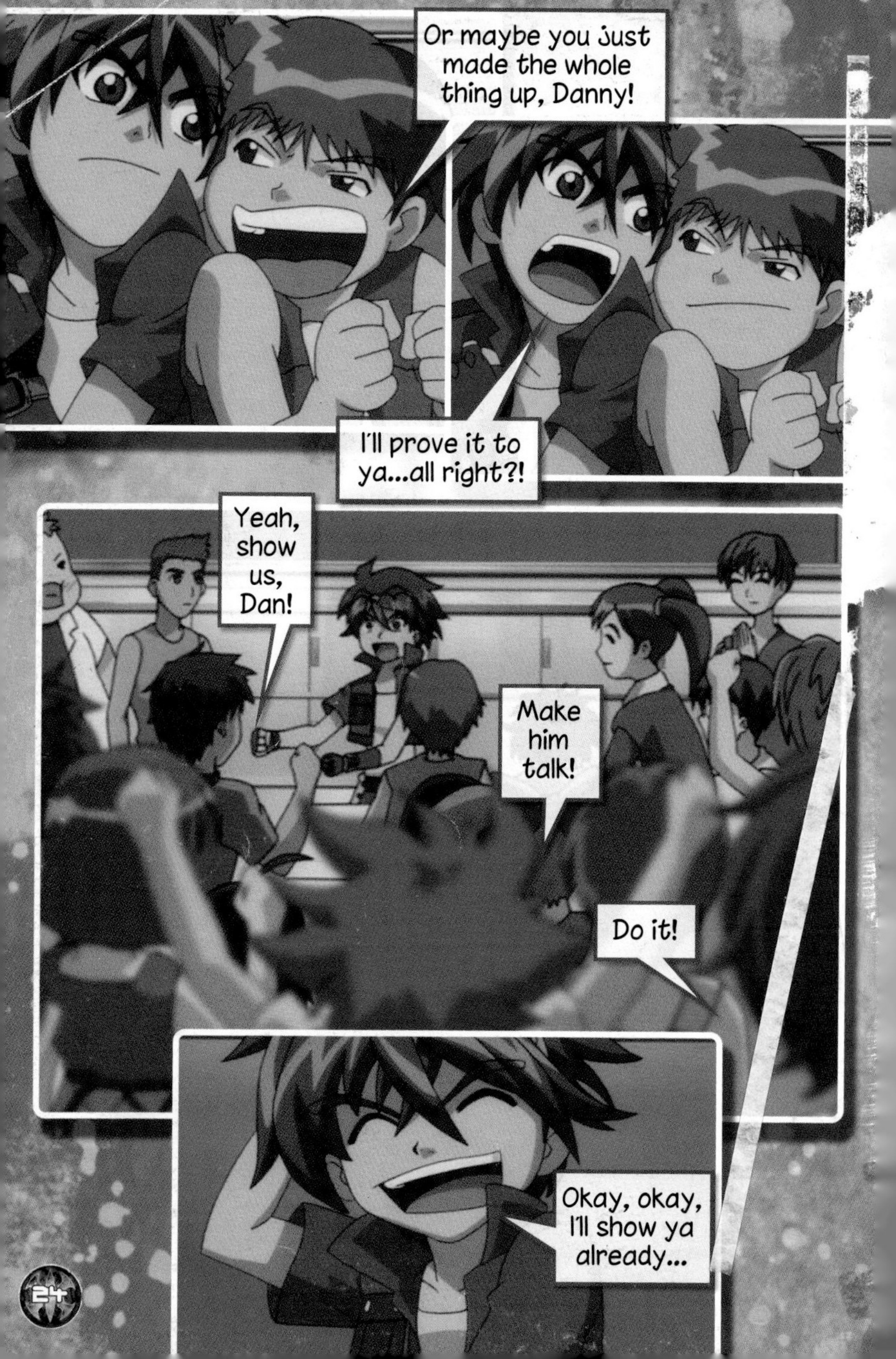
Or maybe you just made the whole thing up, Danny!
I'll prove it to ya...all right?!
Yeah, show us, Dan!
Make him talk!
Do it!
Okay, okay, I'll show ya already...

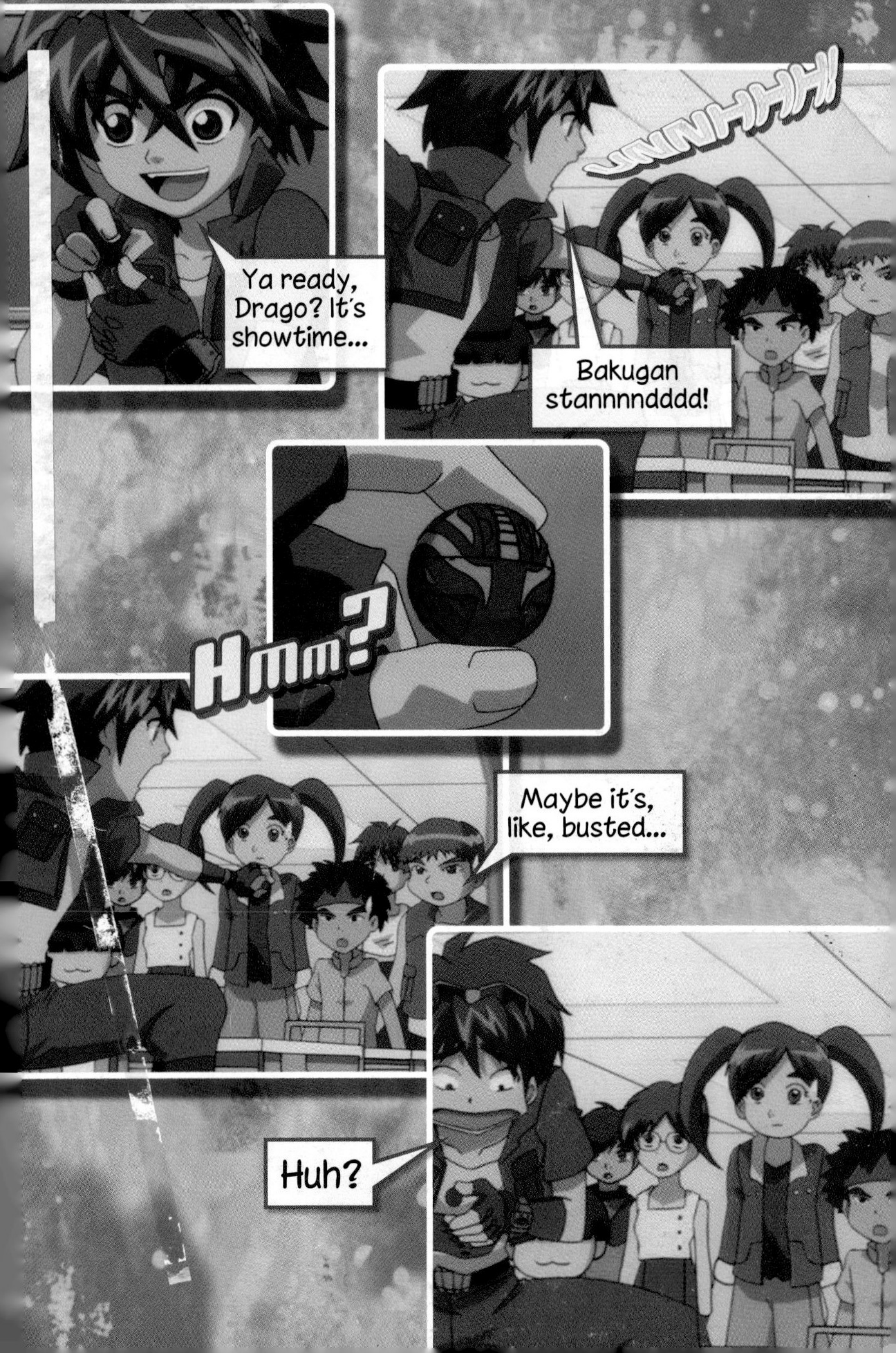
Ya ready, Drago? It's showtime...
VVNHHH!
Bakugan stannnndddd!
Hmm?
Maybe it's, like, busted...
Huh?

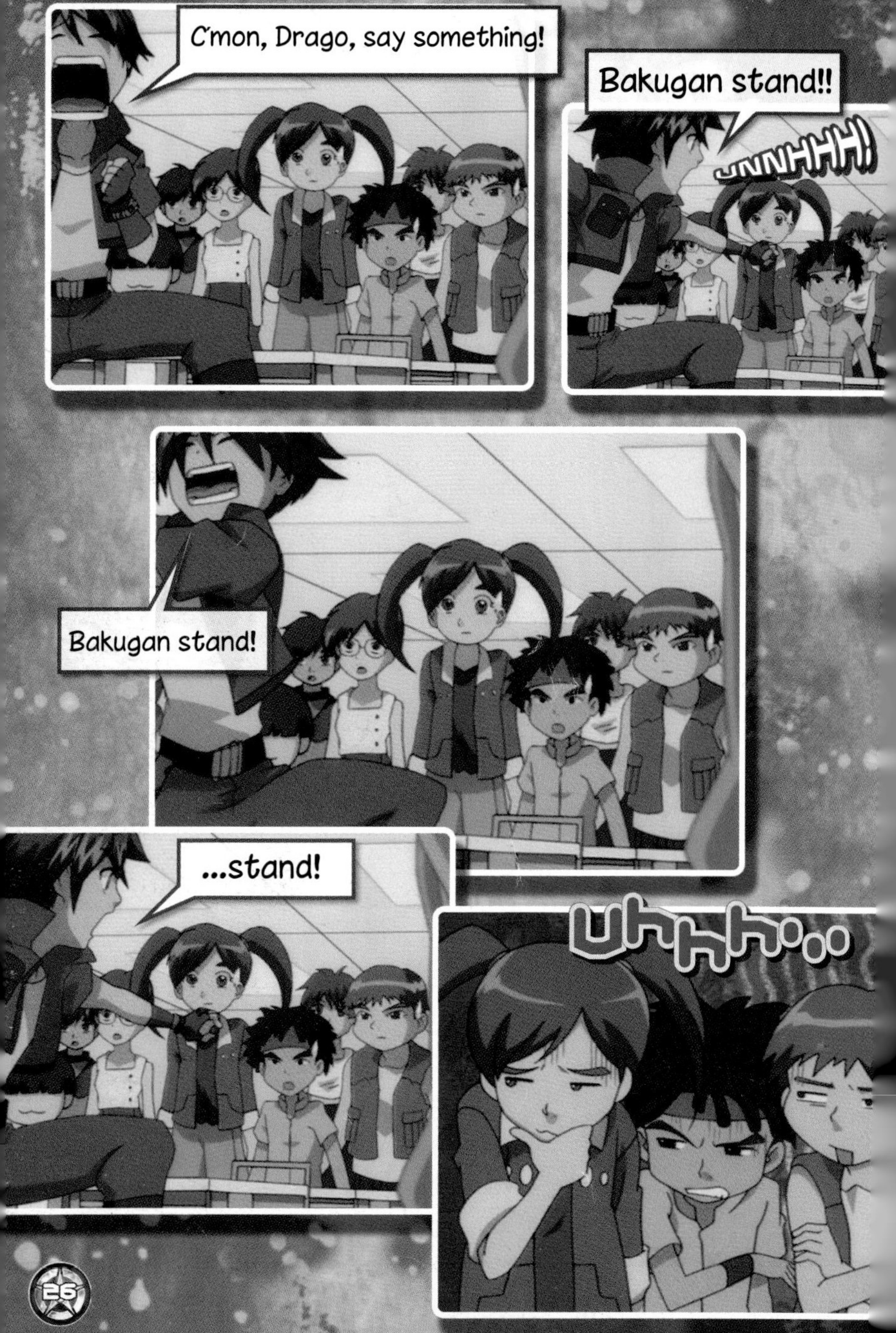
C'mon, Drago, say something!
Bakugan stand!!
UNNHHH!
Bakugan stand!
...stand!
Uhhh..

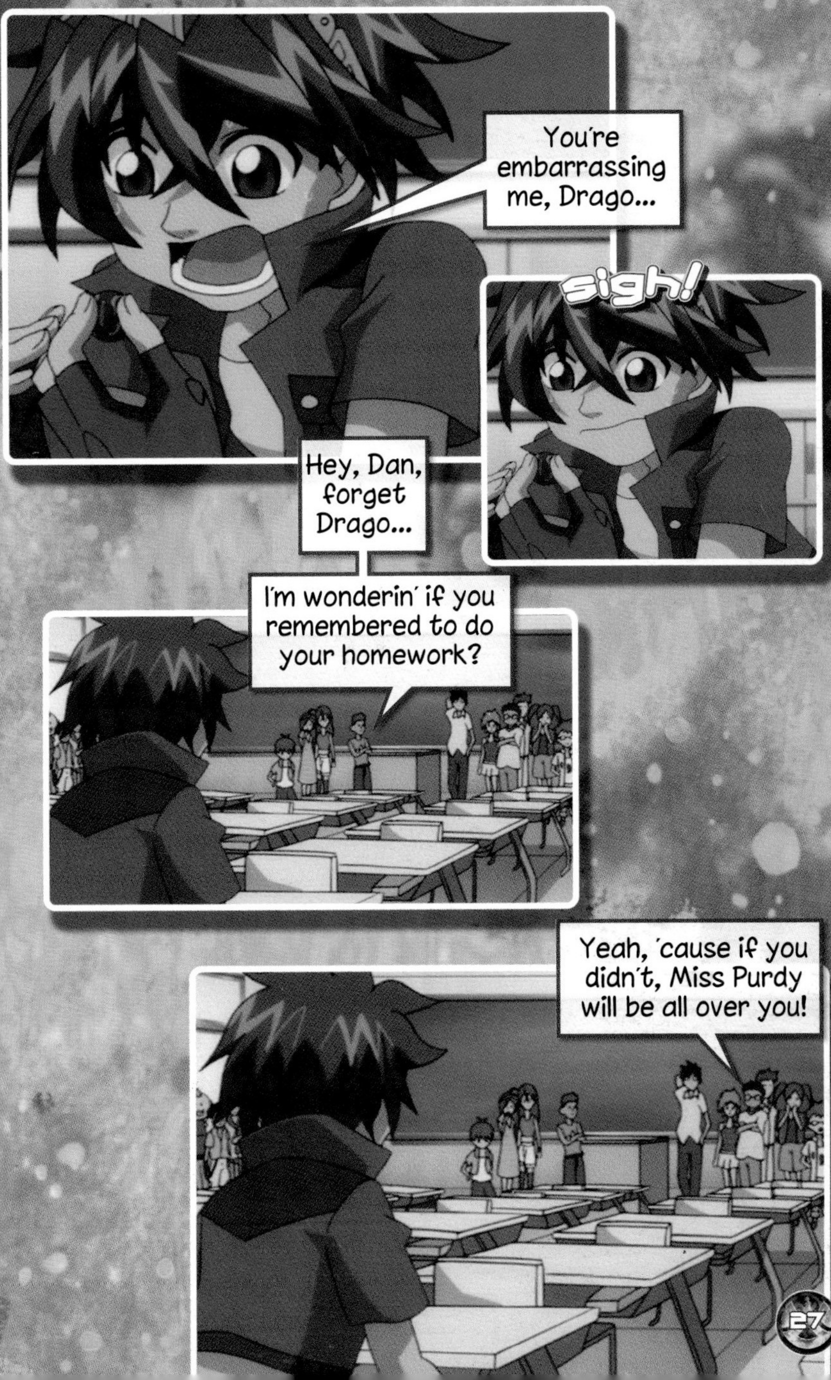
You're embarrassing me, Drago...
sigh!
Hey, Dan, forget Drago...
I'm wonderin' if you remembered to do your homework?
Yeah, 'cause if you didn't, Miss Purdy will be all over you!

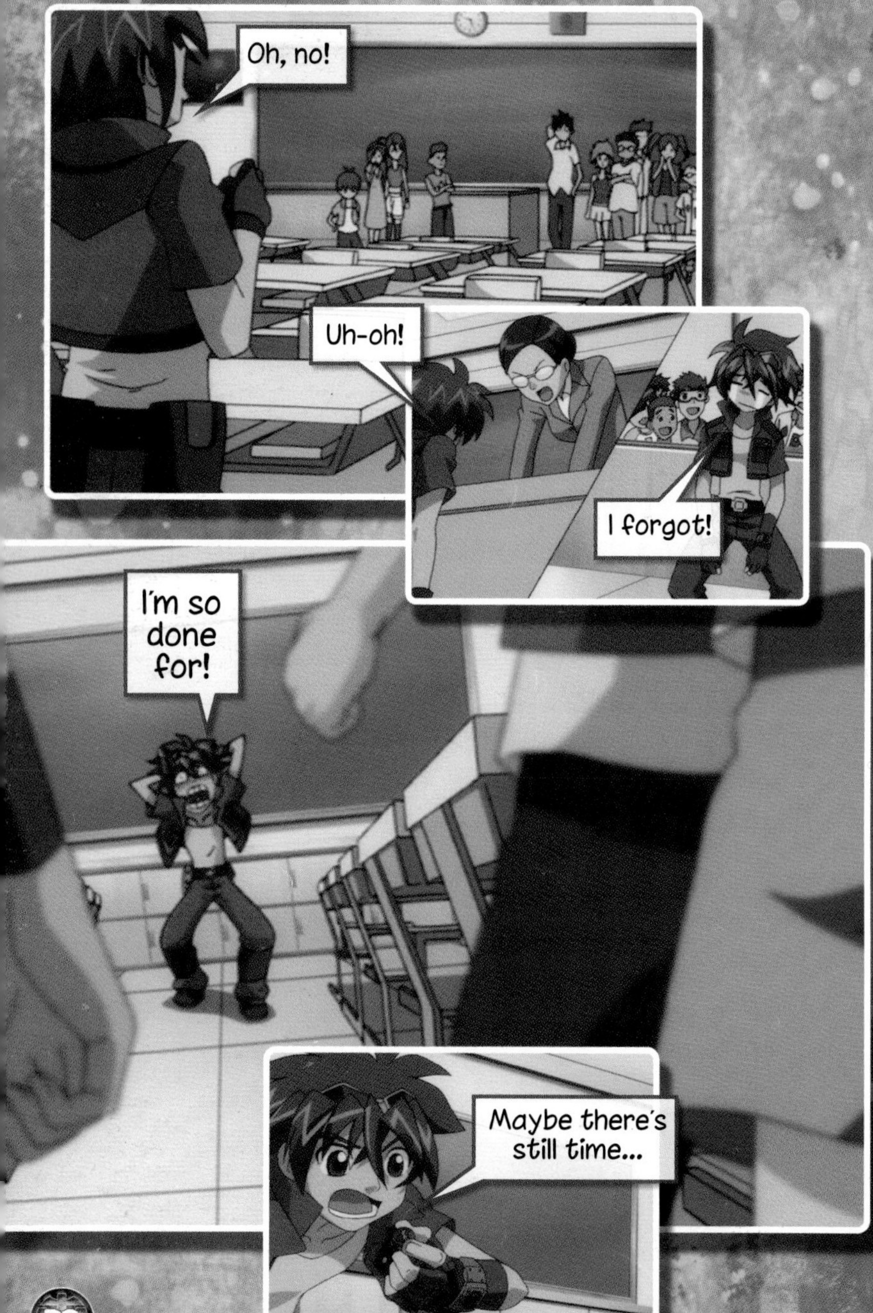
Oh, no!
Uh-oh!
I forgot!
I'm so done for!
Maybe there's still time...

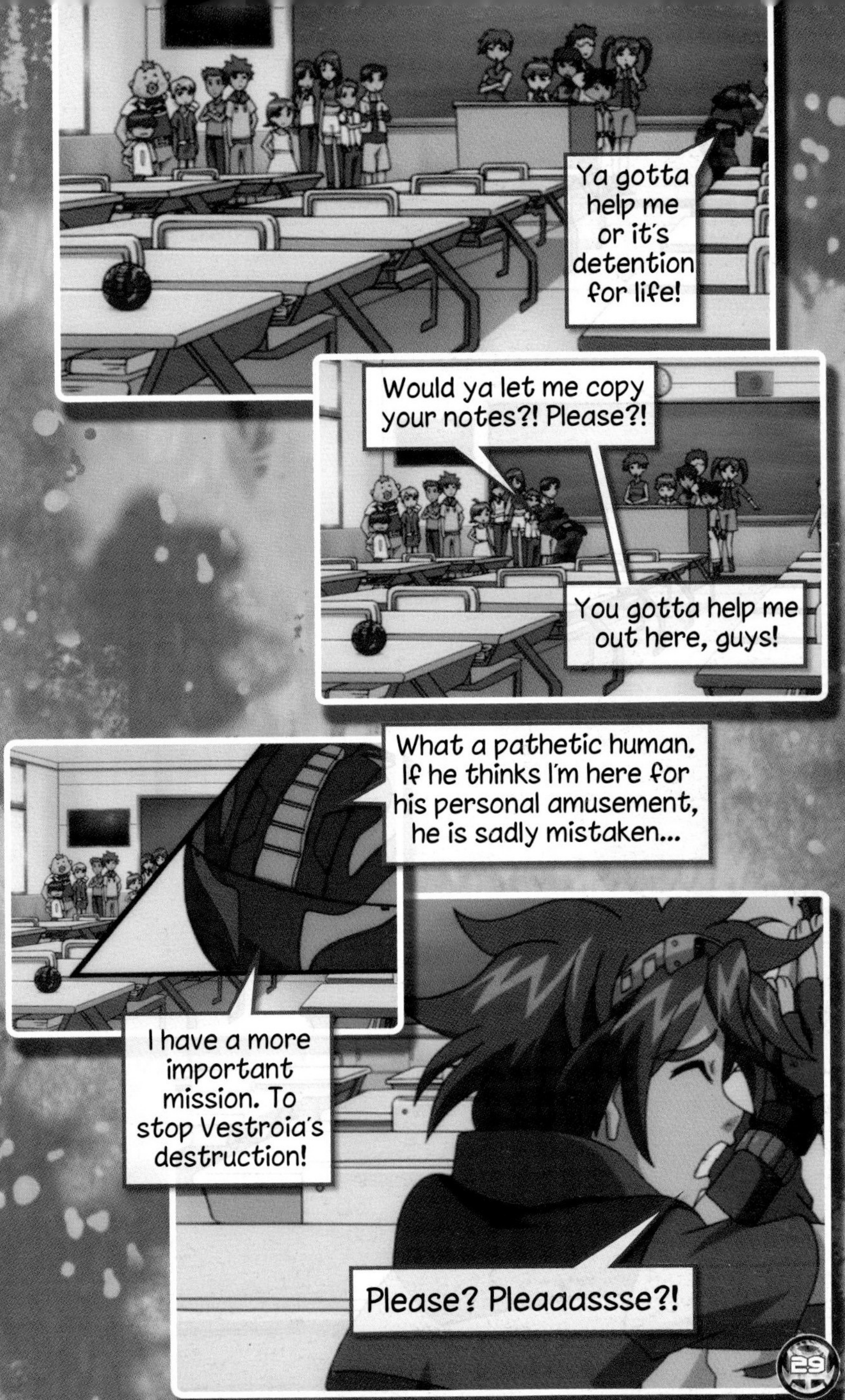
Ya gotta help me or it's detention for life!
Would ya let me copy your notes?! Please?!
You gotta help me out here, guys!
What a pathetic human. If he thinks I'm here for his personal amusement, he is sadly mistaken...
I have a more important mission. To stop Vestroia's destruction!
Please? Pleaaassse?!

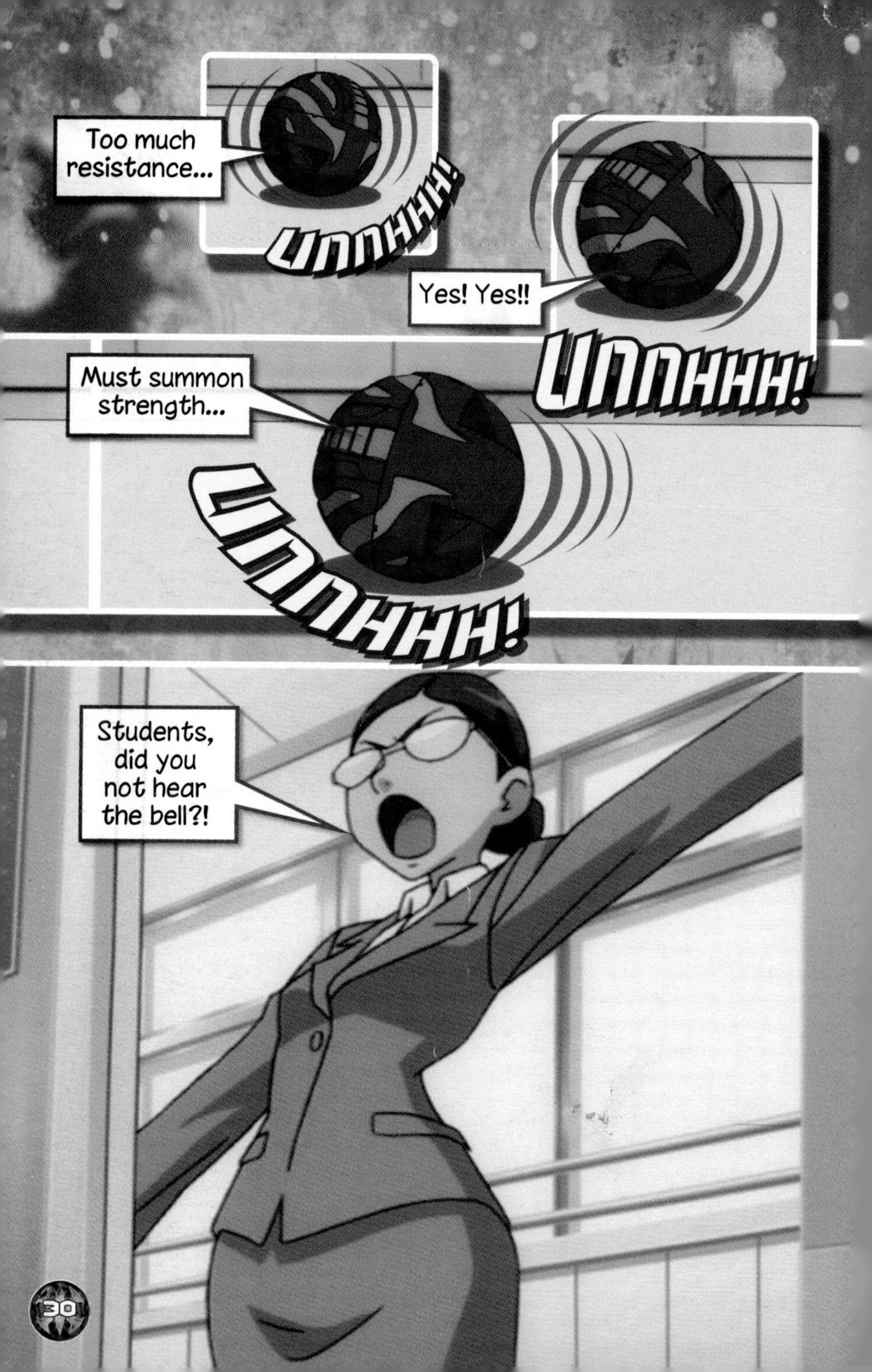

Too much resistance...
UNNHHH!
Yes! Yes!!
UNNHHH!
Must summon strength...
UNNHHH!
Students, did you not hear the bell?!

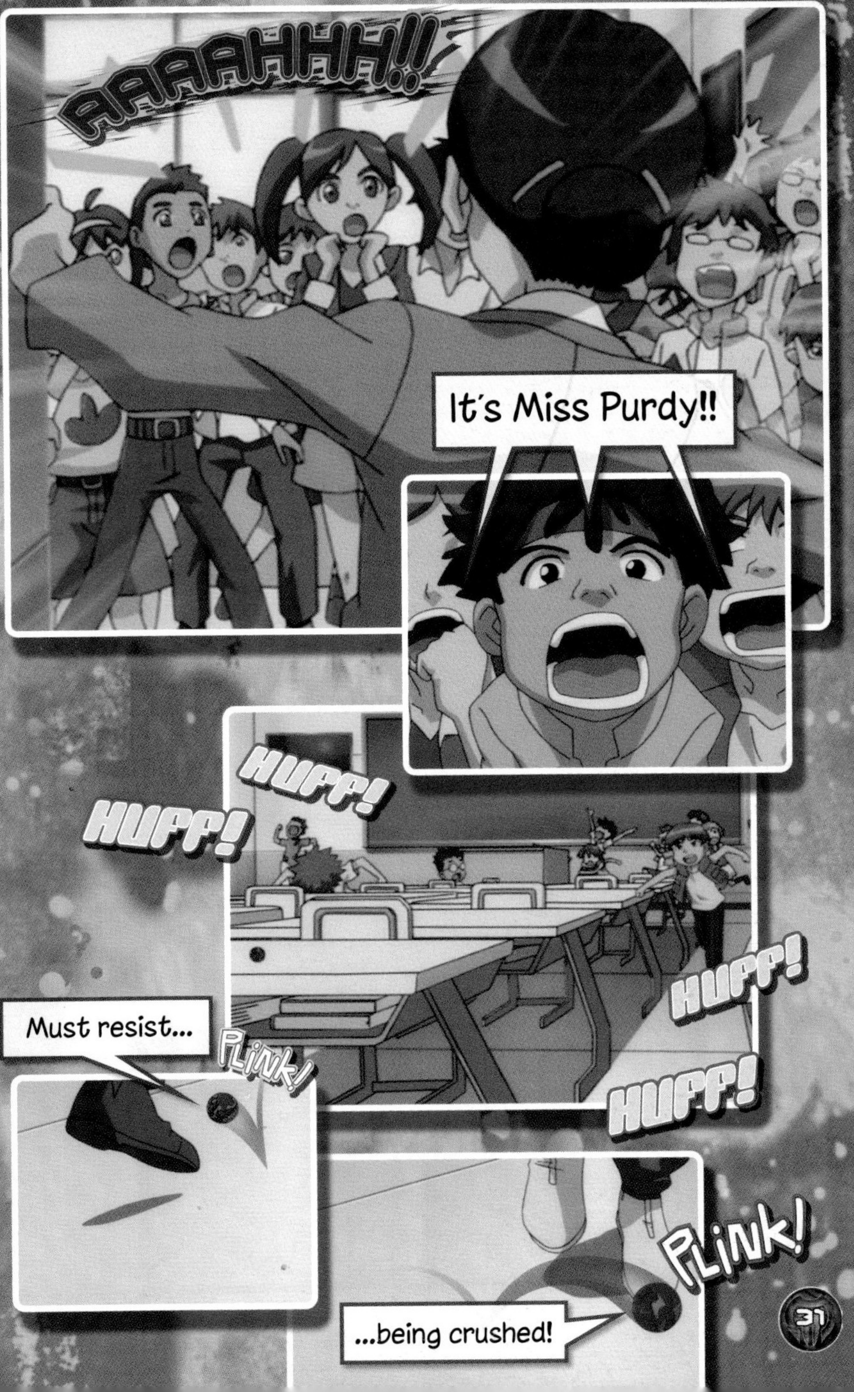
AAAAHHH!!
It's Miss Purdy!!
HUFF!
HUFF!
HUFF!
HUFF!
Must resist...
PLINK!
PLINK!
...being crushed!

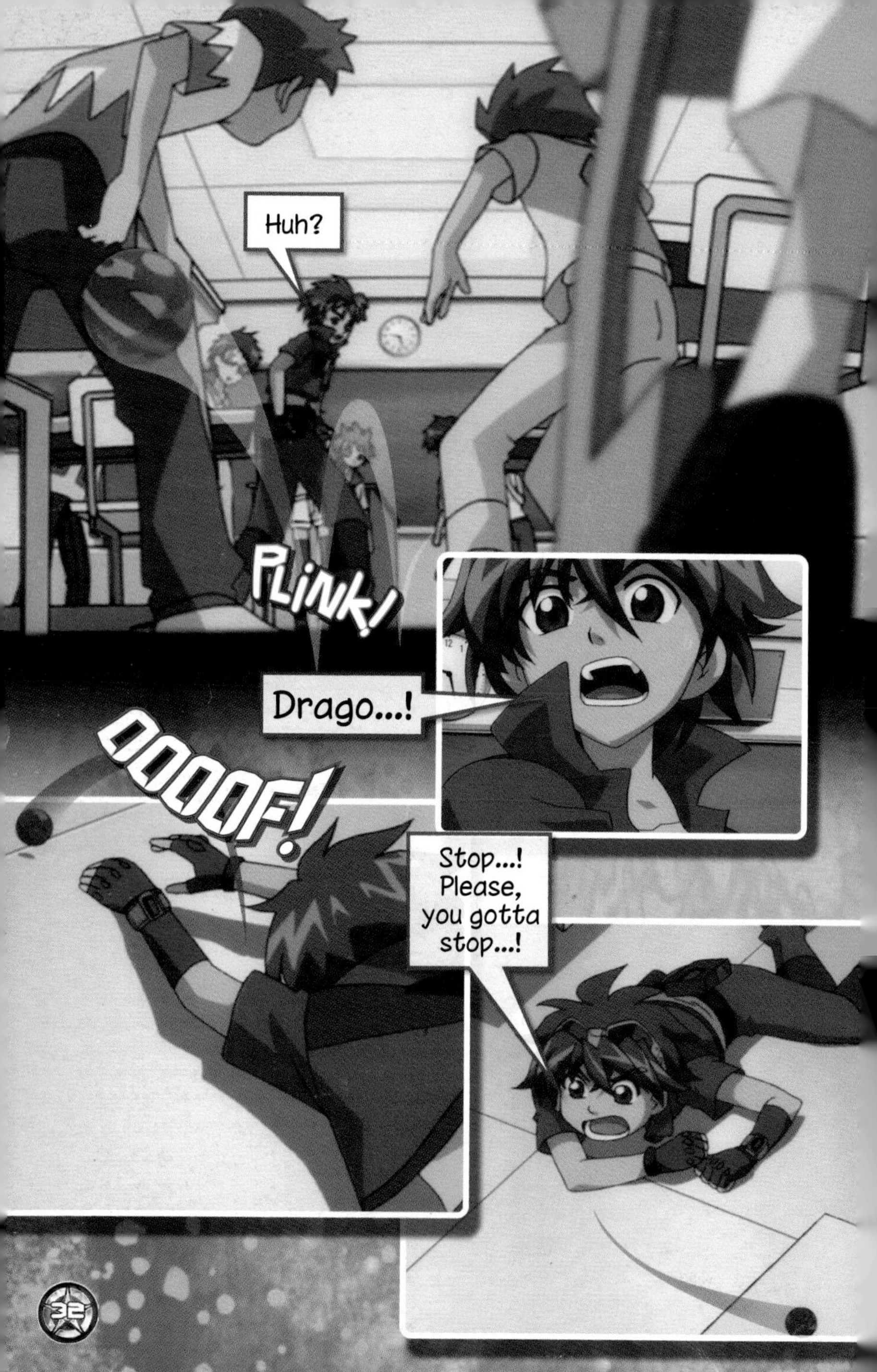
Huh?
PLINK!
Drago...!
OOOOF!
Stop...! Please, you gotta stop...!

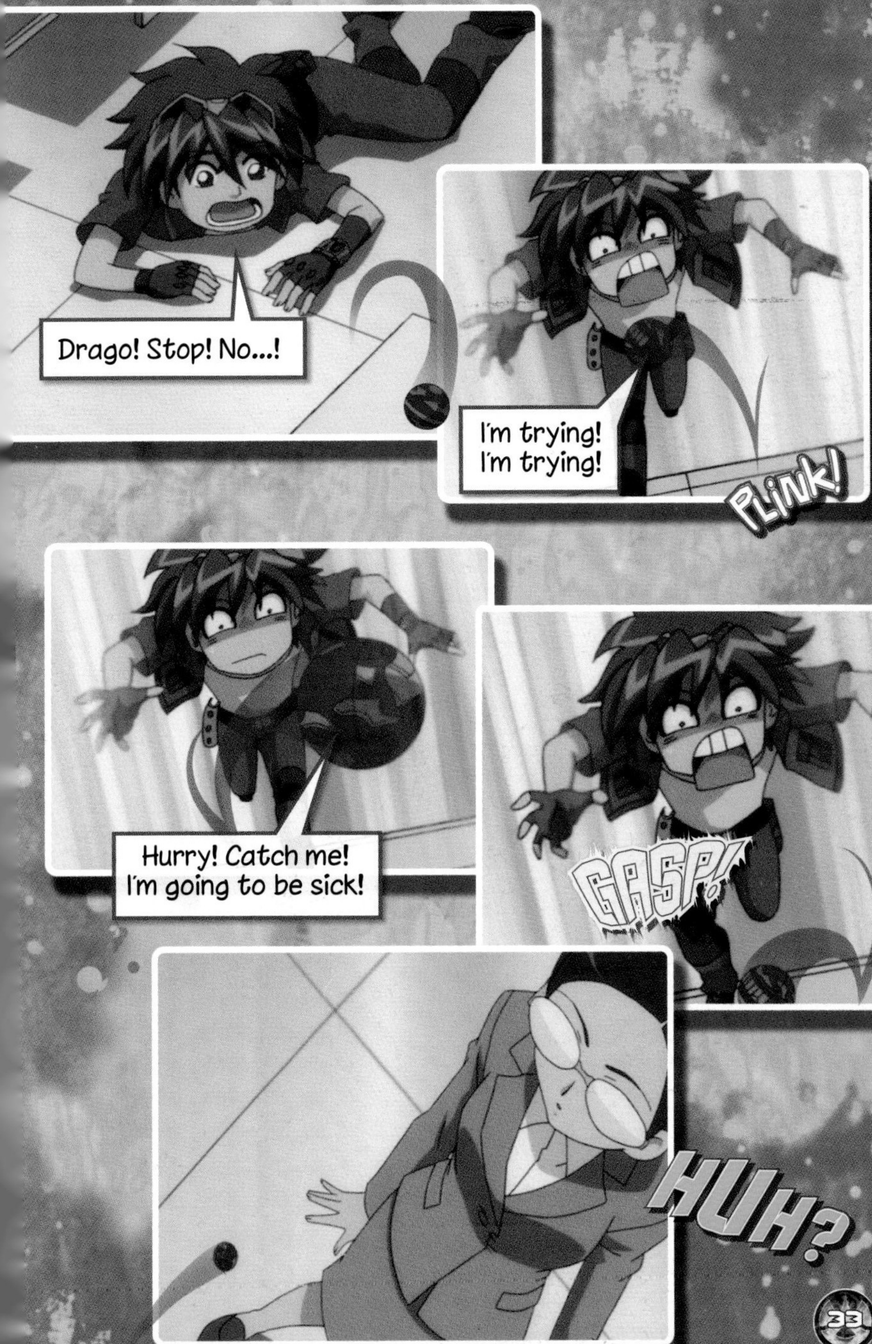
Drago! Stop! No...!
I'm trying! I'm trying!
PLINK!
Hurry! Catch me! I'm going to be sick!
GASP!
HUH?

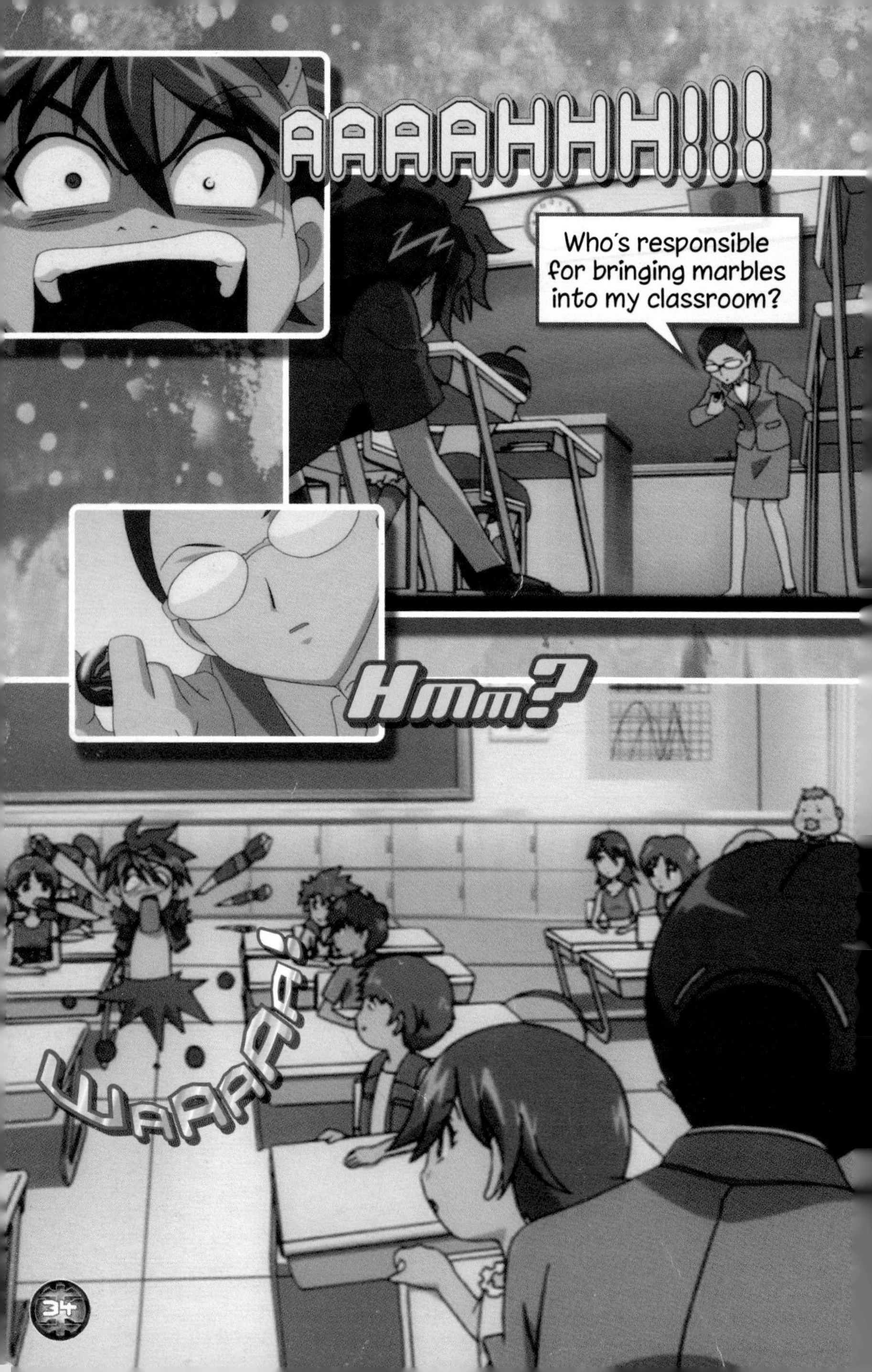
AAAAHHH!!!
Who's responsible for bringing marbles into my classroom?
Hmm?
WAAAA

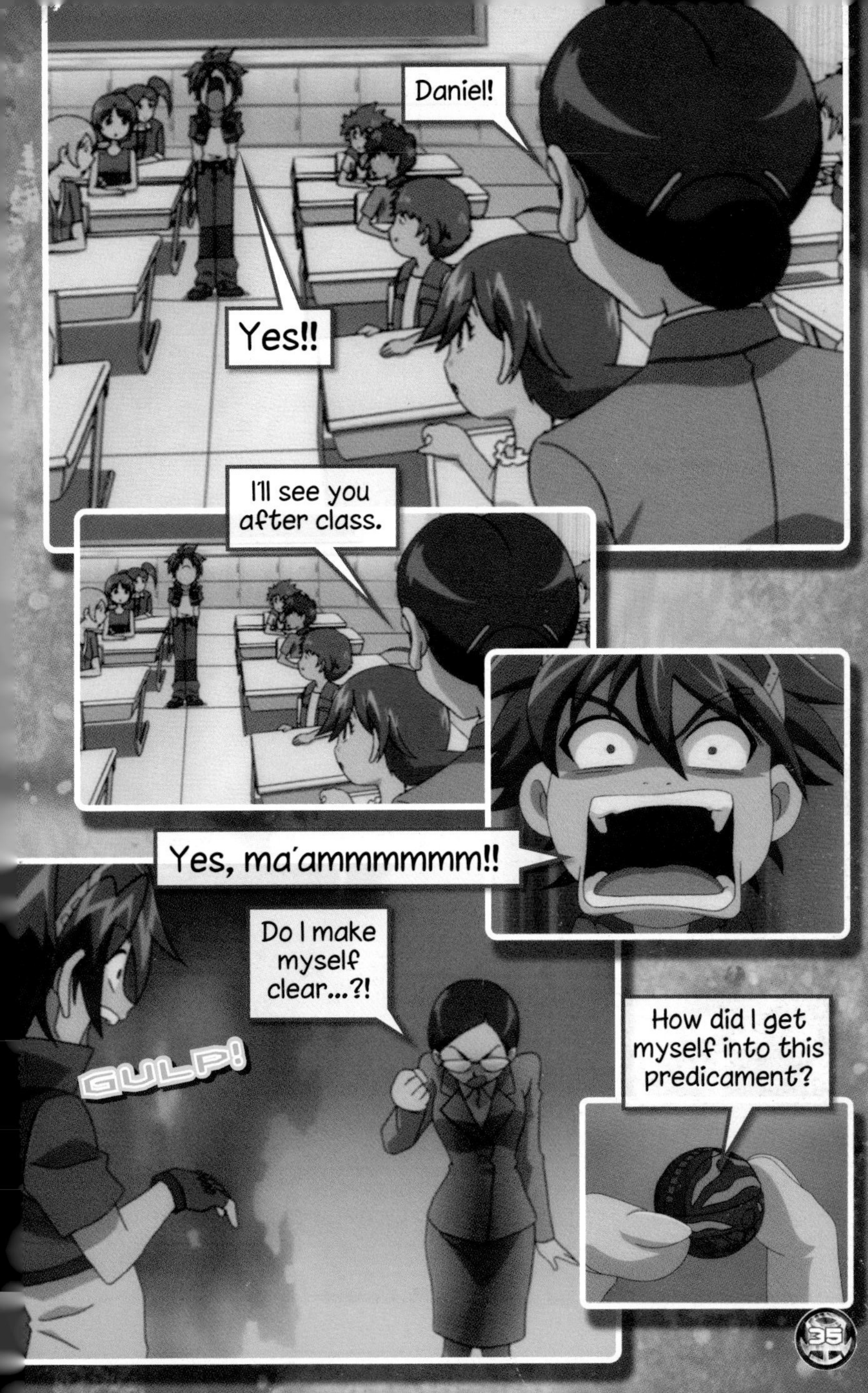
Daniel!
Yes!!
I'll see you after class.
Yes, ma'ammmmmm!!
Do I make myself clear...?!
GULP!
How did I get myself into this predicament?

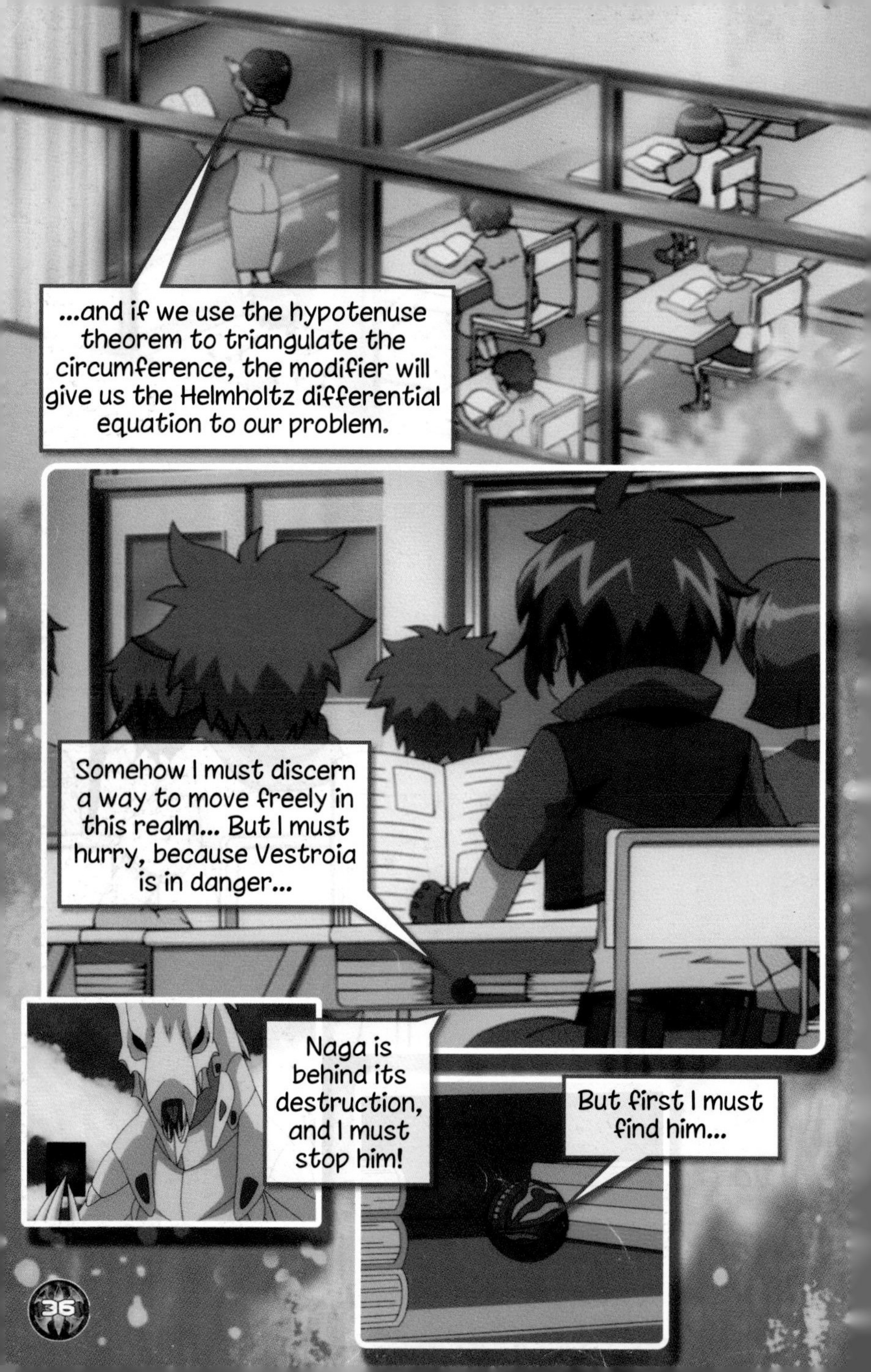
...and if we use the hypotenuse theorem to triangulate the circumference, the modifier will give us the Helmholtz differential equation to our problem.
Somehow I must discern a way to move freely in this realm... But I must hurry, because Vestroia is in danger...
Naga is behind its destruction, and I must stop him!
But first I must find him...

Reaching into his desk, Dan picks up Drago...

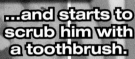

...and starts to scrub him with a toothbrush.

HUH?

BRUUUSH

BRUUUSH

Ah, man, all that rollin' around on the floor sure messed you up, little guy. There. Now you're starting to look like new again...

BRUUUUSH

BRUUUUSH

I'll bet you're wishing I'd do this all day, and if you'd just talk for me, well, maybe I might..

BRUUUUSH

Hmmph!

BRUUUUSH

Cease your scrubbing, human!!

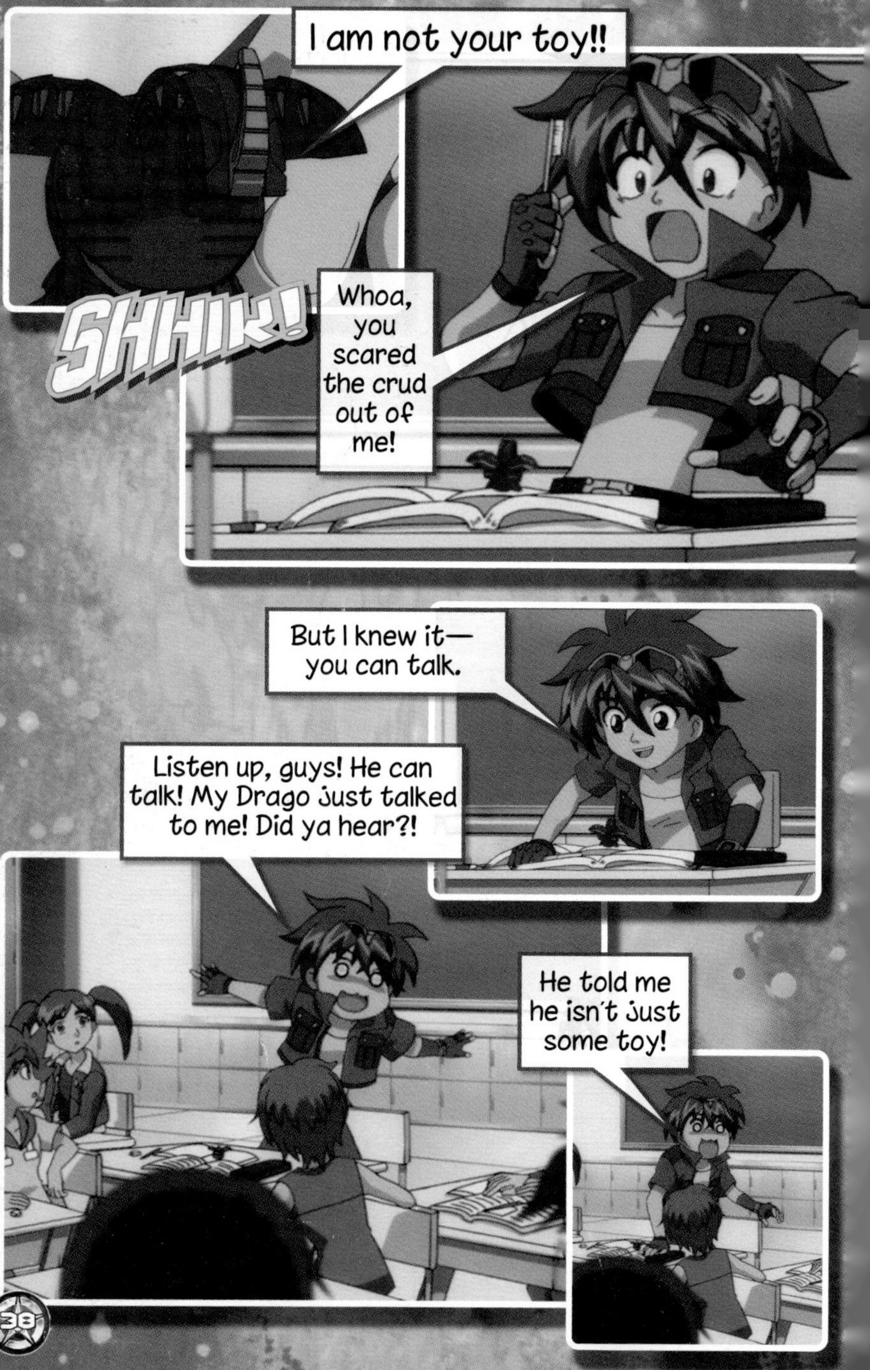
I am not your toy!!
SHHIK!
Whoa, you scared the crud out of me!
But I knew it—you can talk.
Listen up, guys! He can talk! My Drago just talked to me! Did ya hear?!
He told me he isn't just some toy!

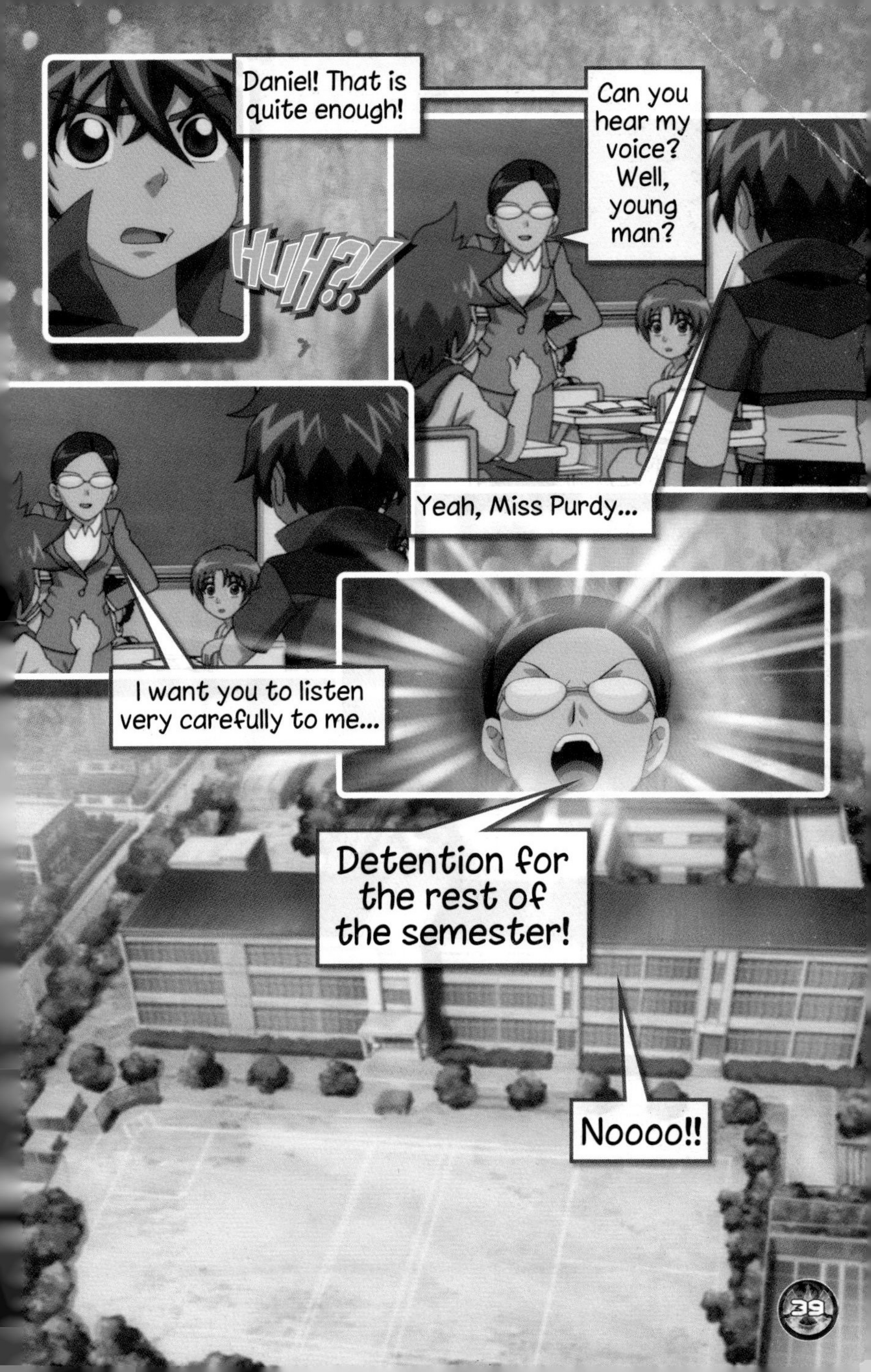
Daniel! That is quite enough!
HUH?!
Can you hear my voice? Well, young man?
Yeah, Miss Purdy...
I want you to listen very carefully to me...
Detention for the rest of the semester!
Noooo!!

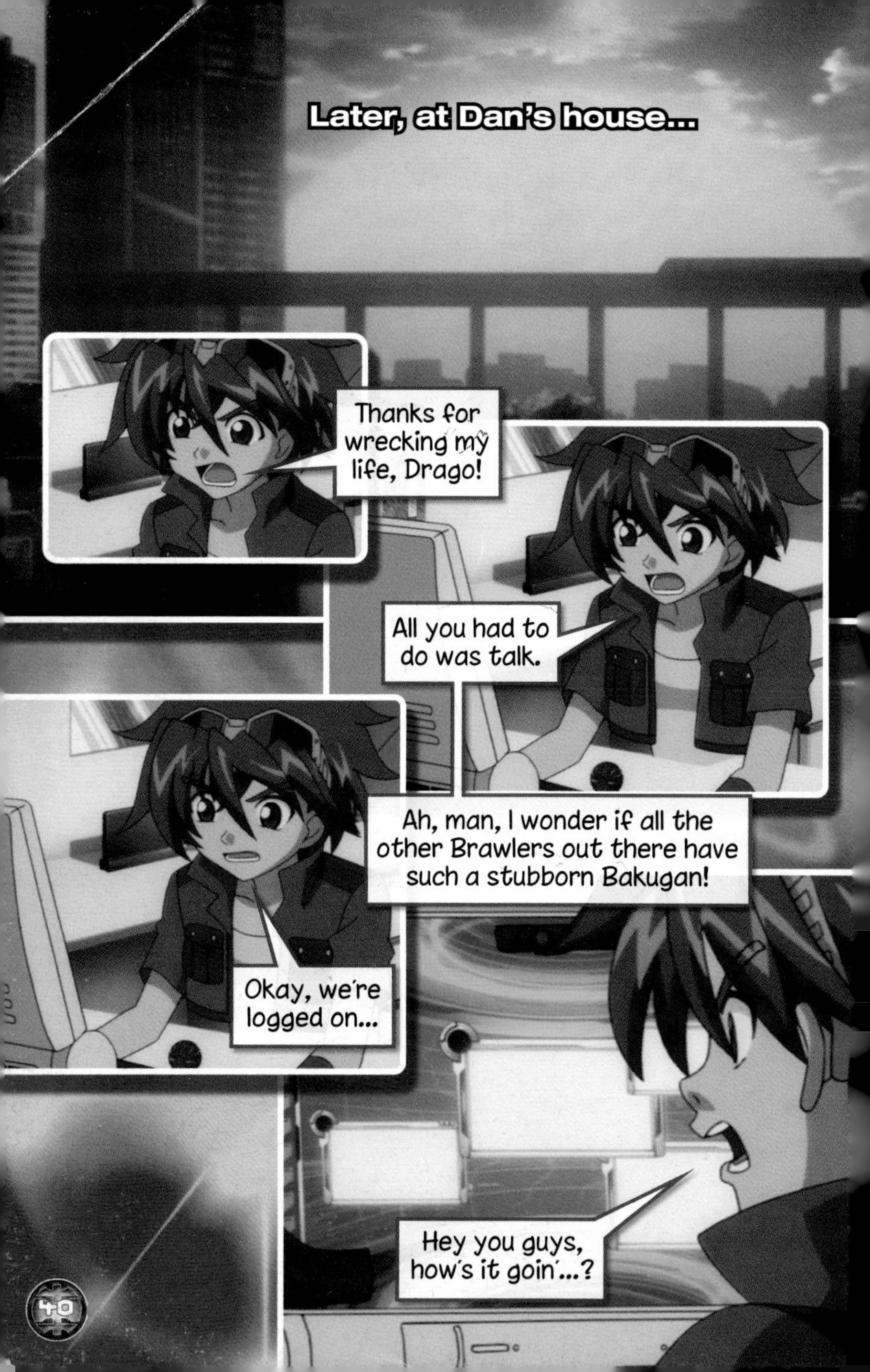

Later, at Dan's house...
Thanks for wrecking my life, Drago!
All you had to do was talk.
Ah, man, I wonder if all the other Brawlers out there have such a stubborn Bakugan!
Okay, we're logged on...
Hey you guys, how's it goin'...?

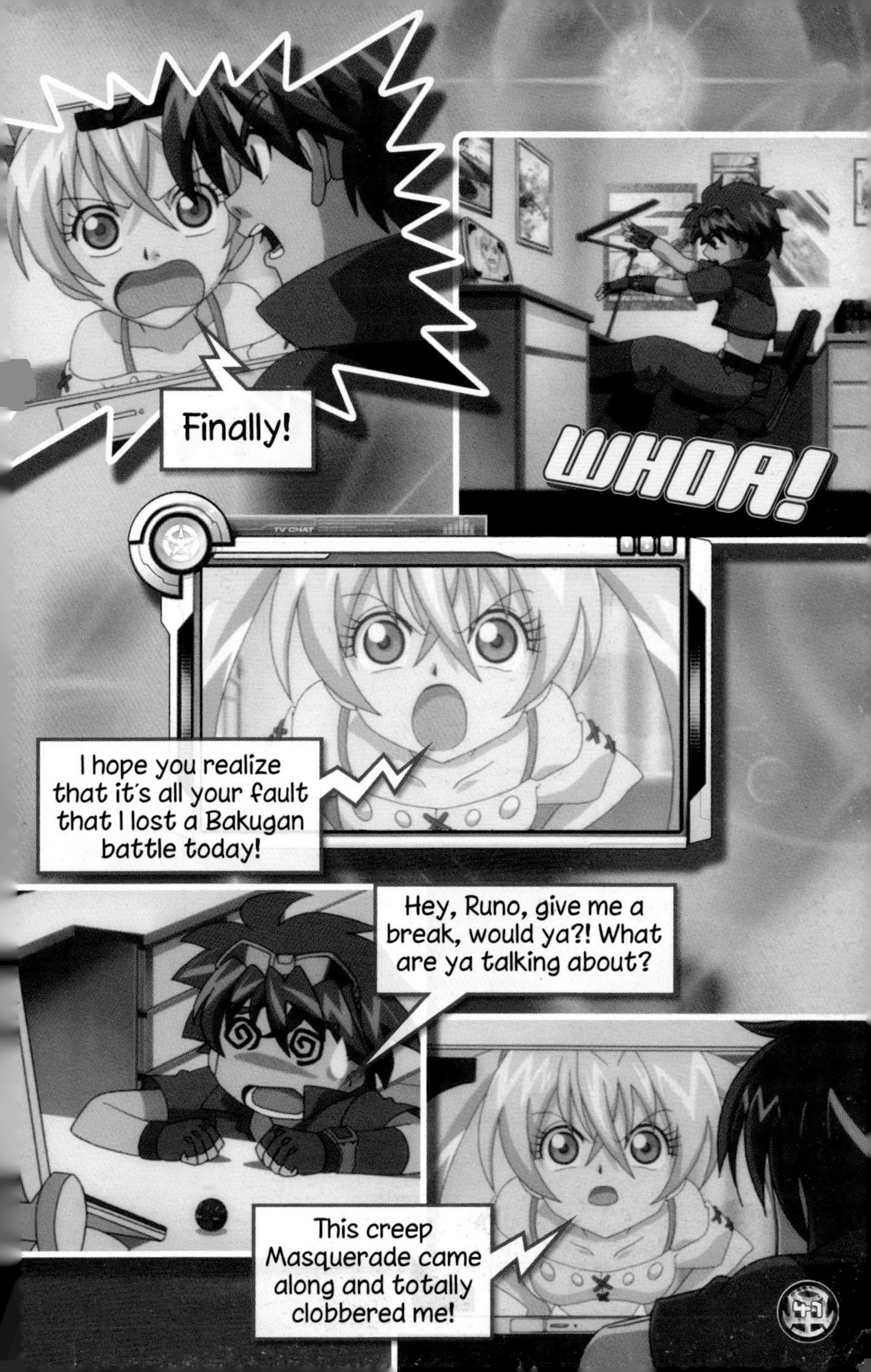
Finally!
WHOA!
TV CHAT
I hope you realize that it's all your fault that I lost a Bakugan battle today!
Hey, Runo, give me a break, would ya?! What are ya talking about?
This creep Masquerade came along and totally clobbered me!
41

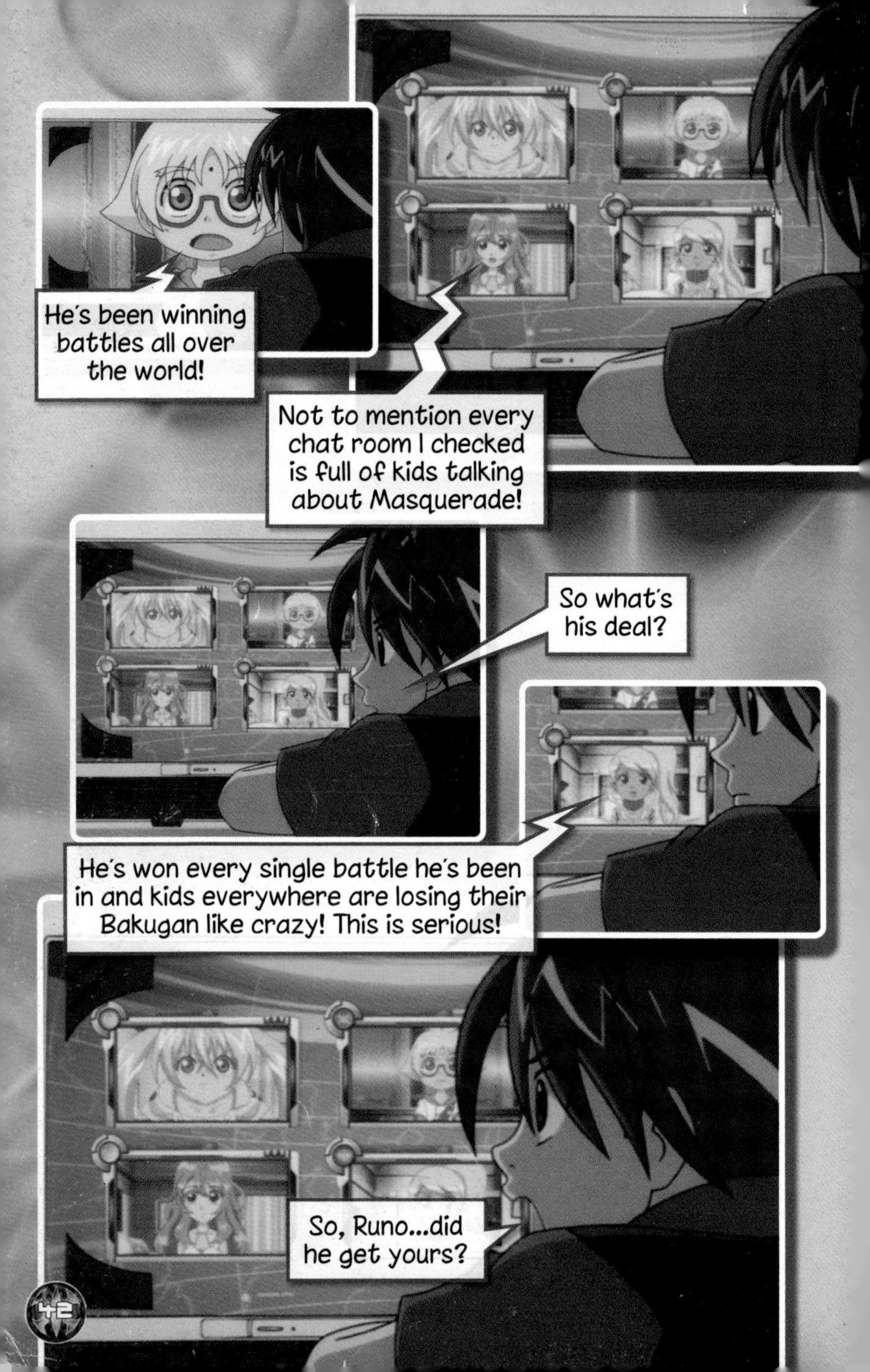
He's been winning battles all over the world!
Not to mention every chat room I checked is full of kids talking about Masquerade!
So what's his deal?
He's won every single battle he's been in and kids everywhere are losing their Bakugan like crazy! This is serious!
So, Runo...did he get yours?

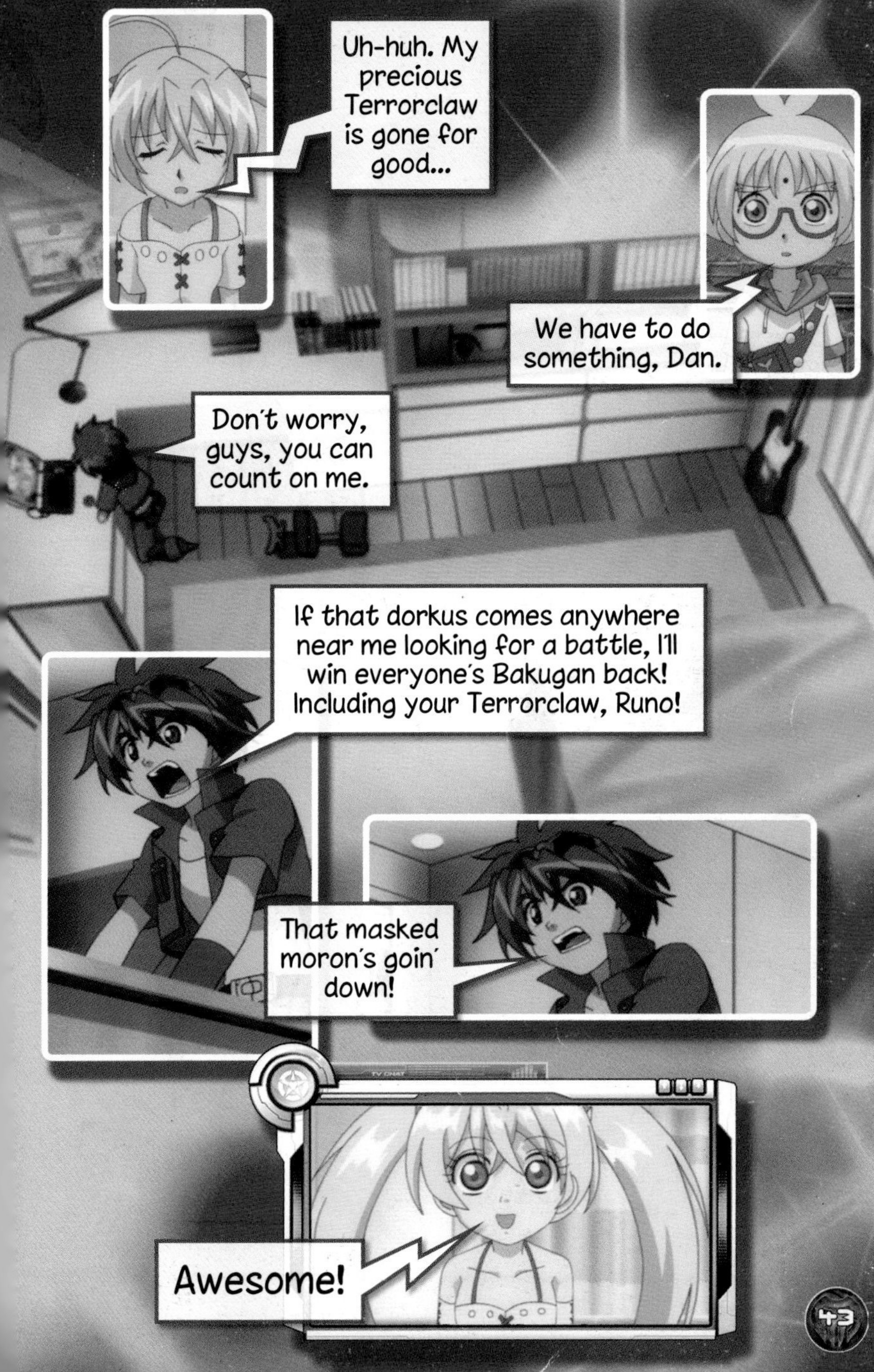
Uh-huh. My precious Terrorclaw is gone for good...
We have to do something, Dan.
Don't worry, guys, you can count on me.
If that dorkus comes anywhere near me looking for a battle, I'll win everyone's Bakugan back! Including your Terrorclaw, Runo!
That masked moron's goin' down!
Awesome!

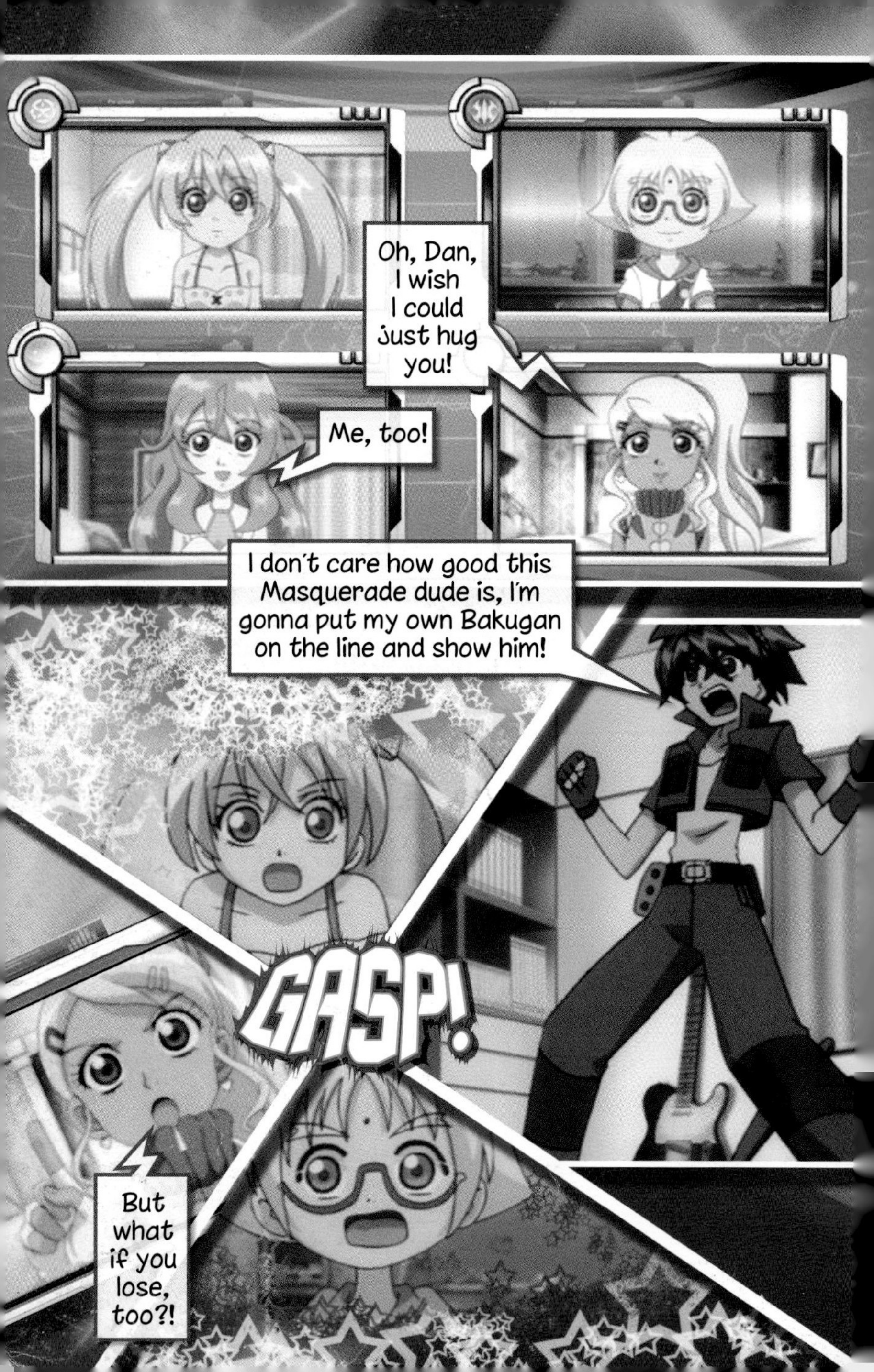
Oh, Dan, I wish I could just hug you!
Me, too!
I don't care how good this Masquerade dude is, I'm gonna put my own Bakugan on the line and show him!
GASP!
But what if you lose, too?!

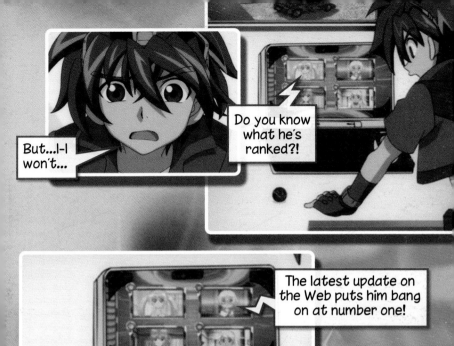

But...I-I won't...

Do you know what he's ranked?!

The latest update on the Web puts him bang on at number one!

You have got to be kiddin'!!

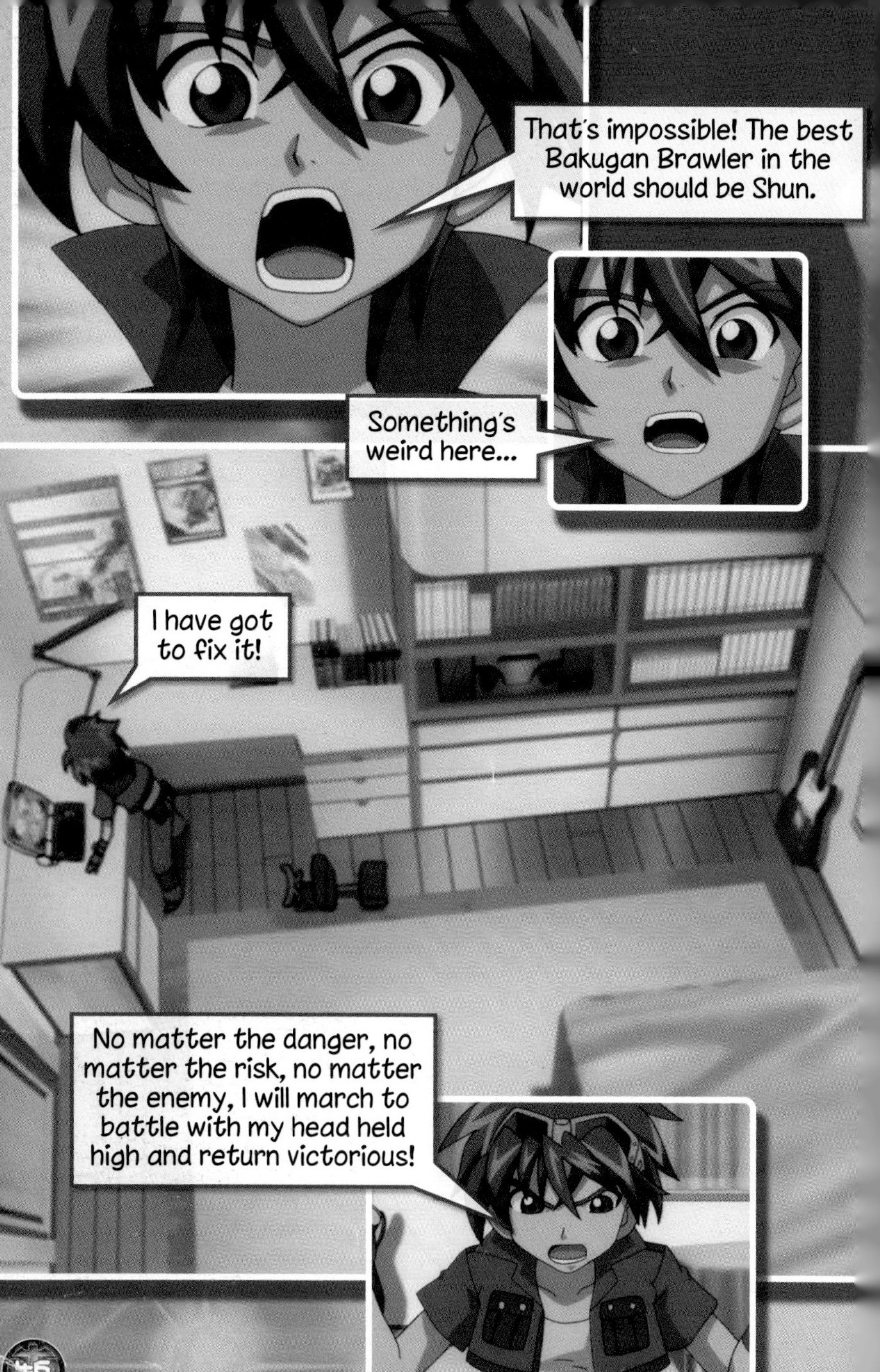
That's impossible! The best Bakugan Brawler in the world should be Shun.
Something's weird here...
I have got to fix it!
No matter the danger, no matter the risk, no matter the enemy, I will march to battle with my head held high and return victorious!

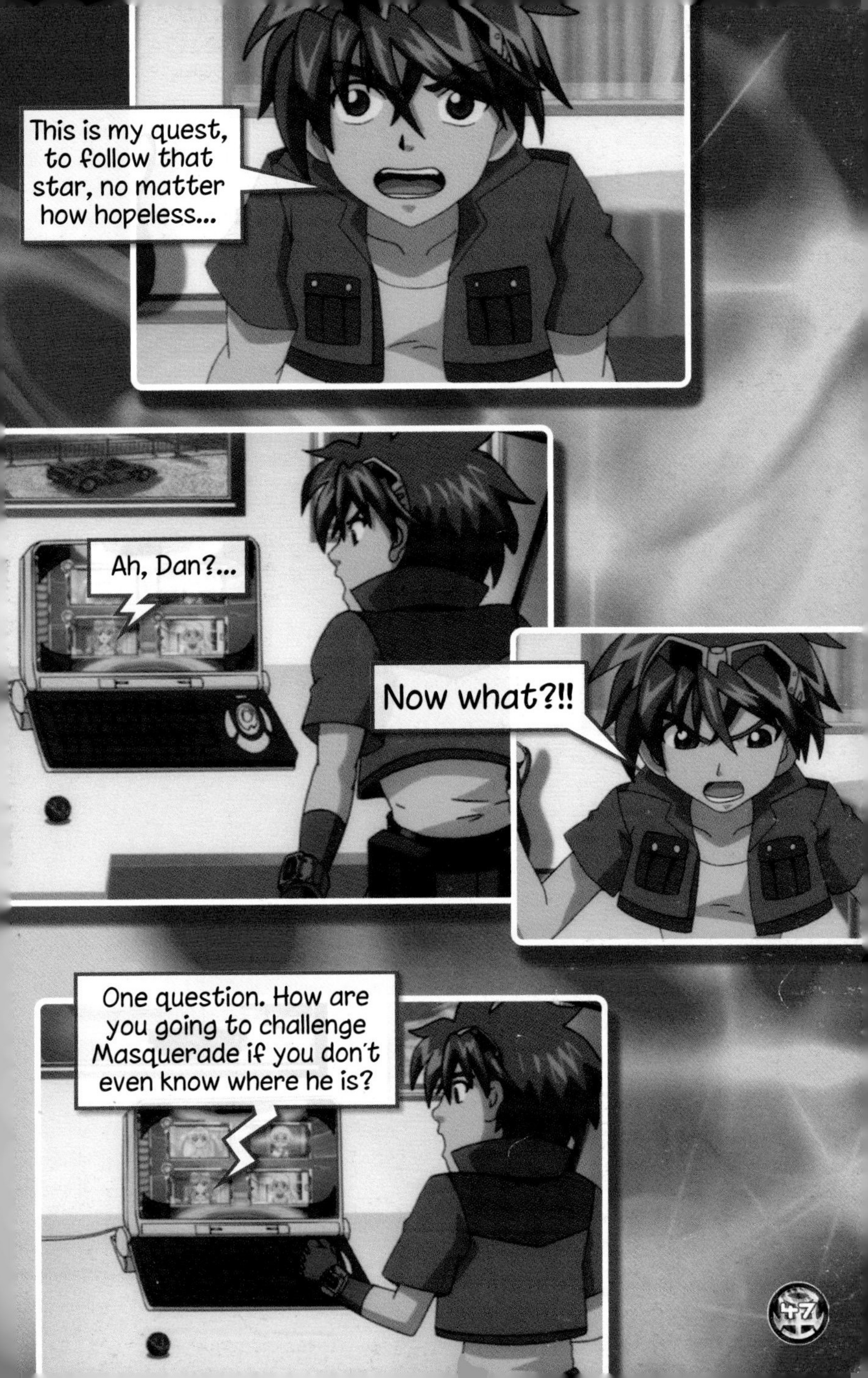
This is my quest, to follow that star, no matter how hopeless...
Ah, Dan?...
Now what?!!
One question. How are you going to challenge Masquerade if you don't even know where he is?

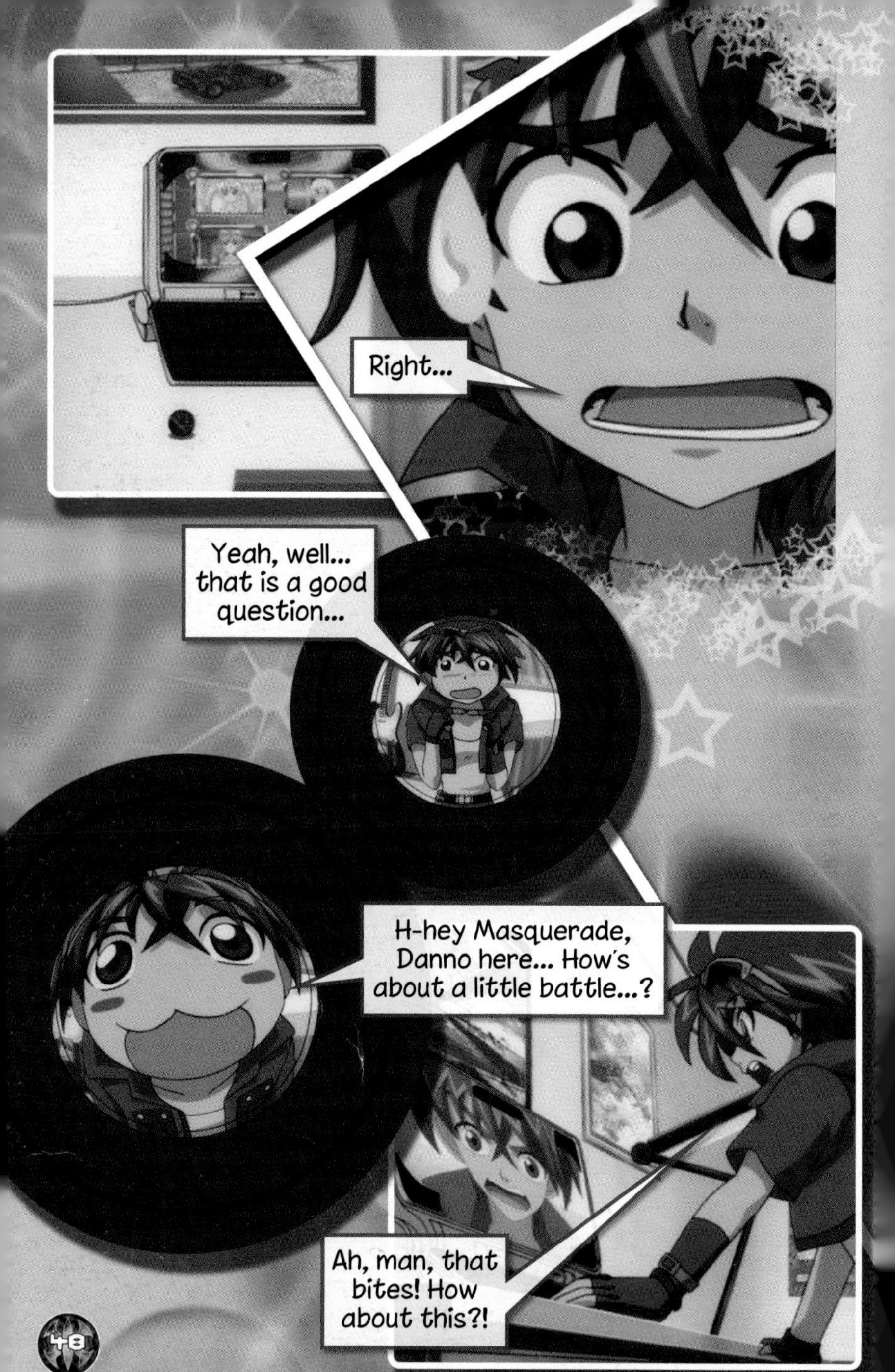
Right...
Yeah, well... that is a good question...
H-hey Masquerade, Danno here... How's about a little battle...?
Ah, man, that bites! How about this?!

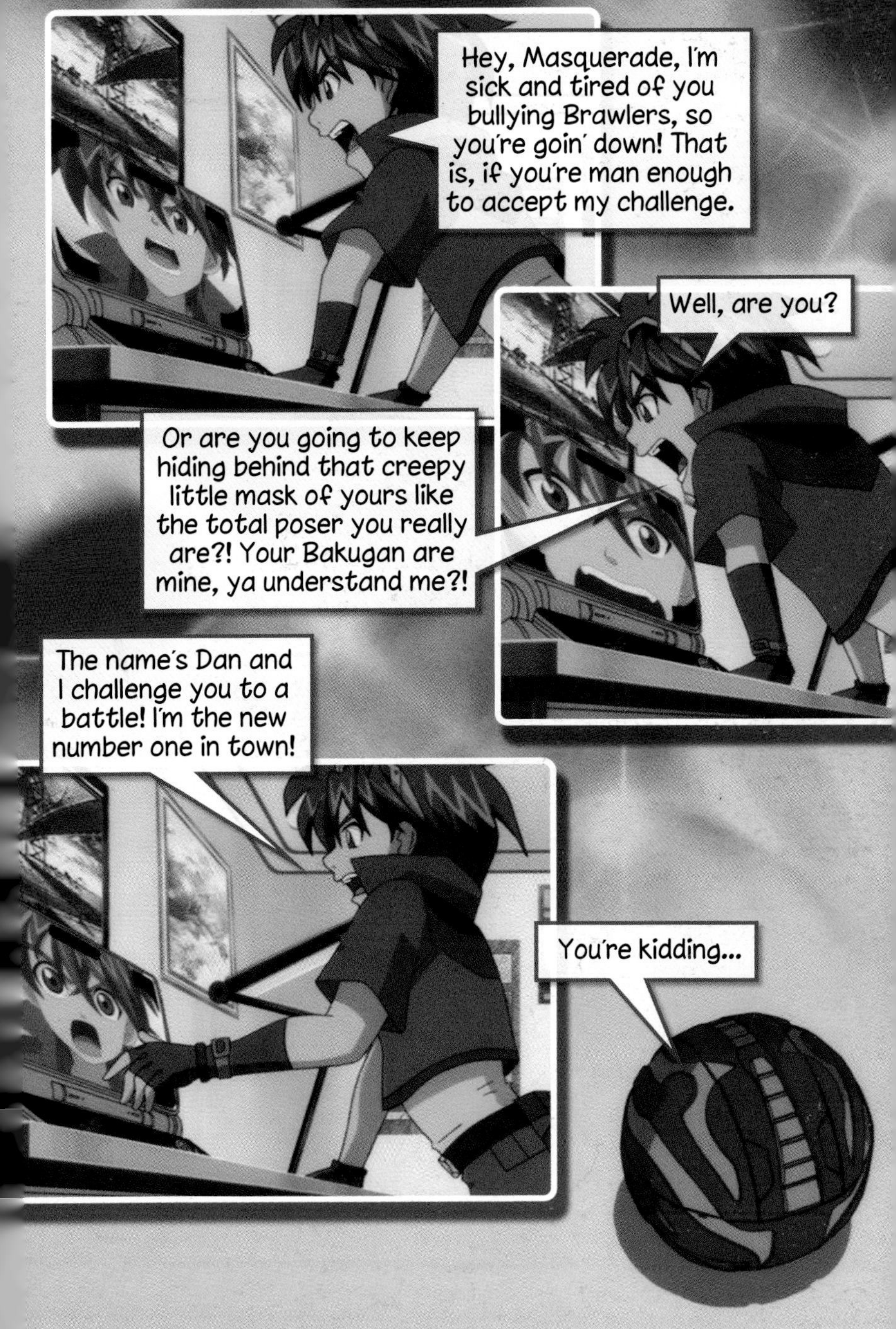
Hey, Masquerade, I'm sick and tired of you bullying Brawlers, so you're goin' down! That is, if you're man enough to accept my challenge.
Well, are you?
Or are you going to keep hiding behind that creepy little mask of yours like the total poser you really are?! Your Bakugan are mine, ya understand me?!
The name's Dan and I challenge you to a battle! I'm the new number one in town!
You're kidding...

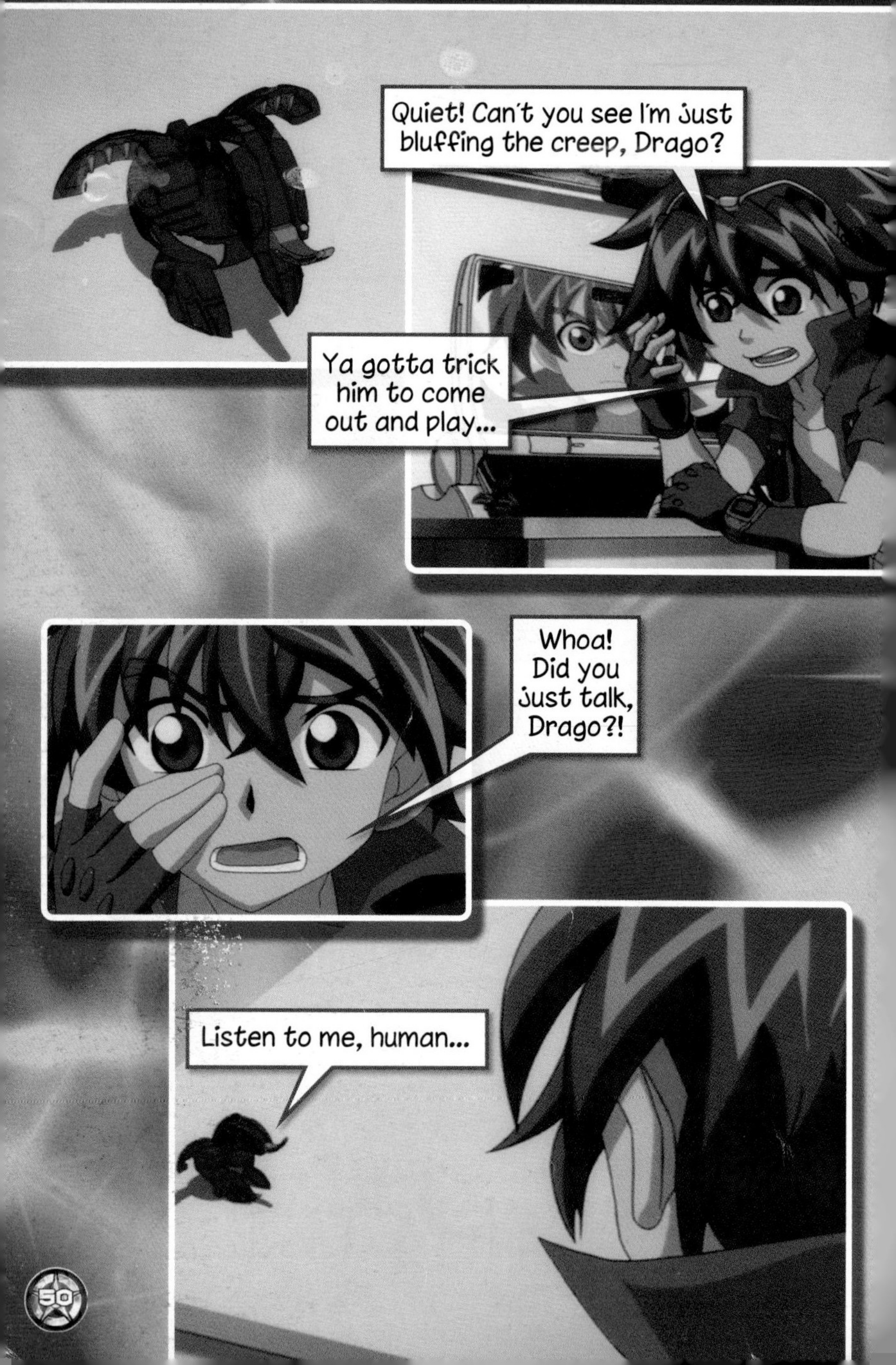
Quiet! Can't you see I'm just bluffing the creep, Drago?
Ya gotta trick him to come out and play...
Whoa! Did you just talk, Drago?!
Listen to me, human...

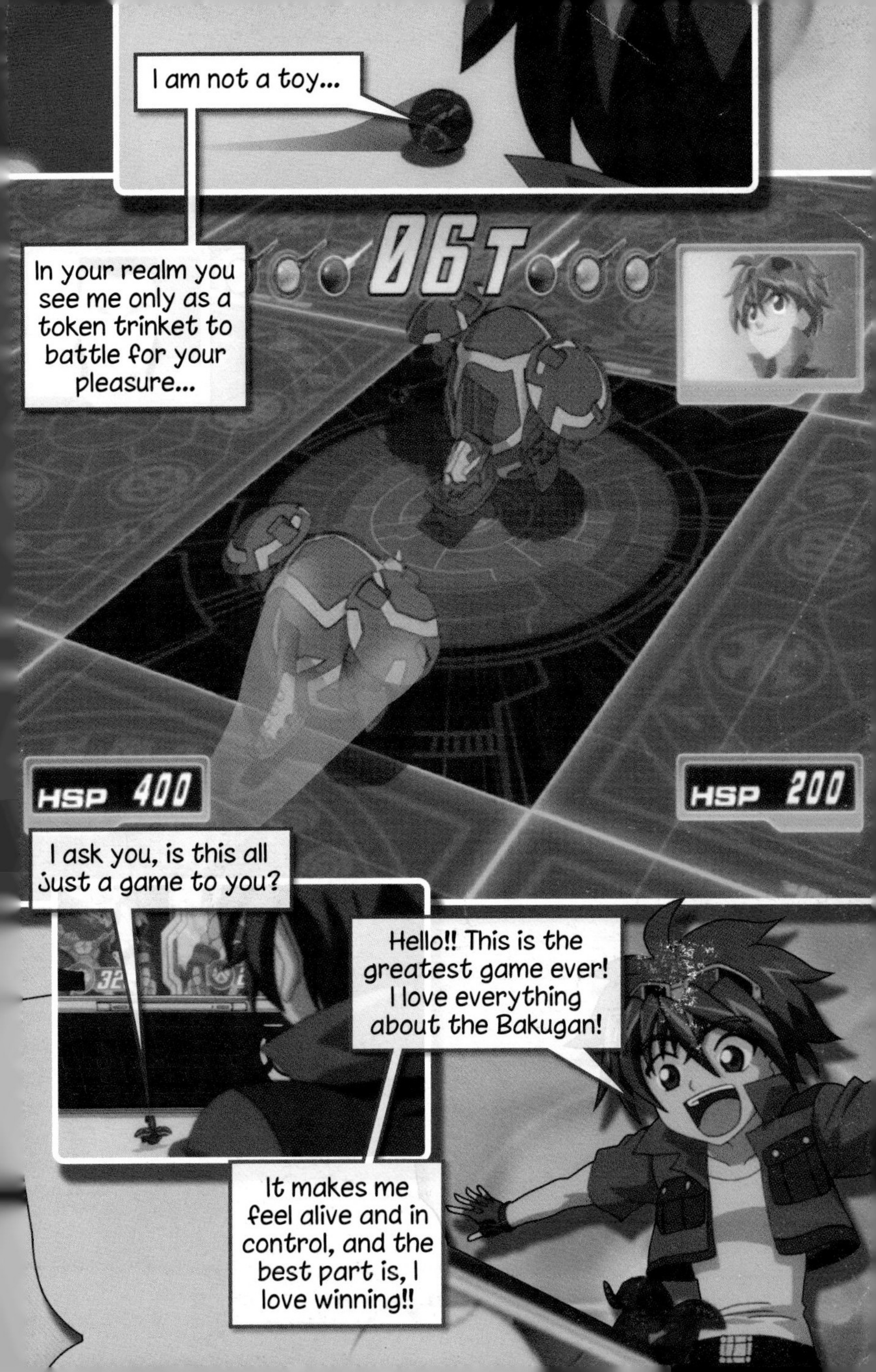
I am not a toy...
In your realm you see me only as a token trinket to battle for your pleasure...
06T
HSP 400
HSP 200
I ask you, is this all just a game to you?
Hello!! This is the greatest game ever! I love everything about the Bakugan!
It makes me feel alive and in control, and the best part is, I love winning!!

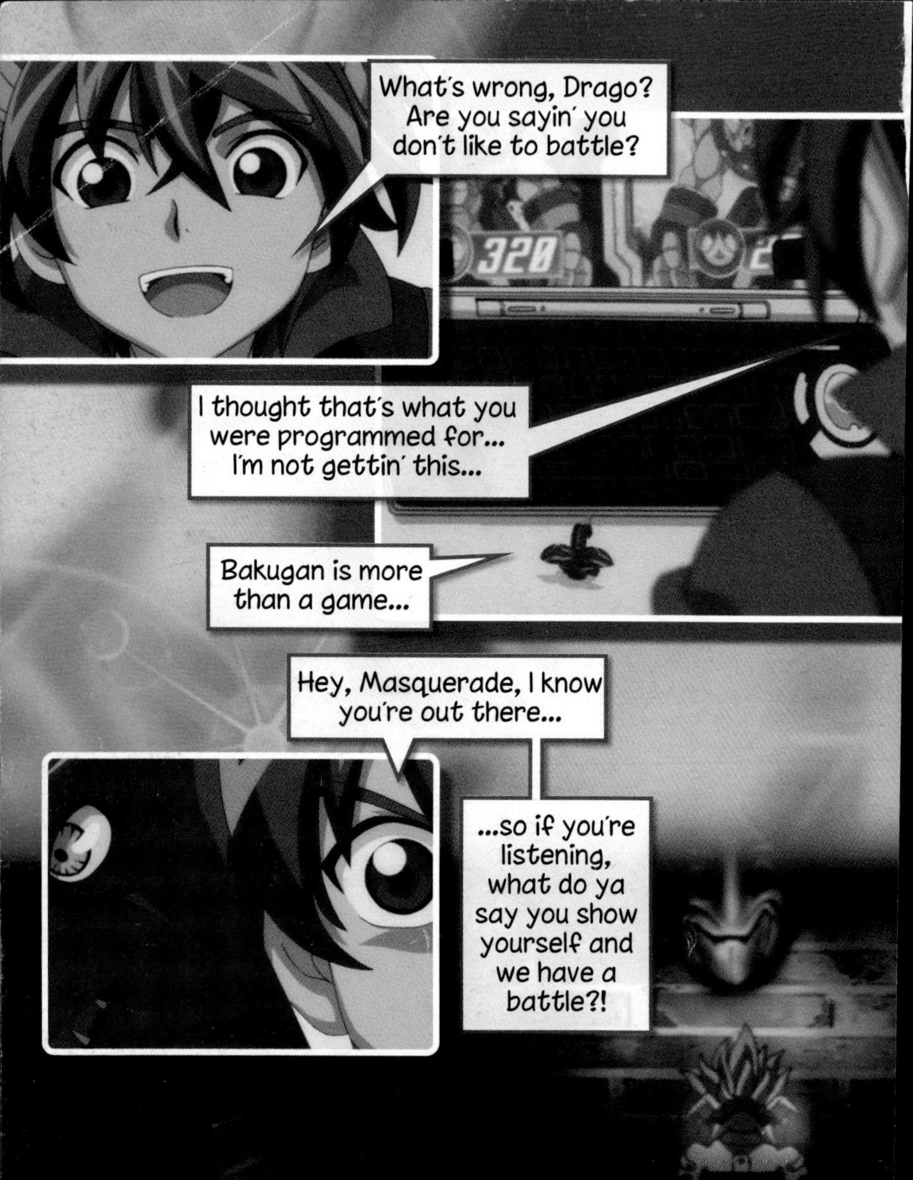
What's wrong, Drago? Are you sayin' you don't like to battle?
320
I thought that's what you were programmed for... I'm not gettin' this...
Bakugan is more than a game...
Hey, Masquerade, I know you're out there...
...so if you're listening, what do ya say you show yourself and we have a battle?!

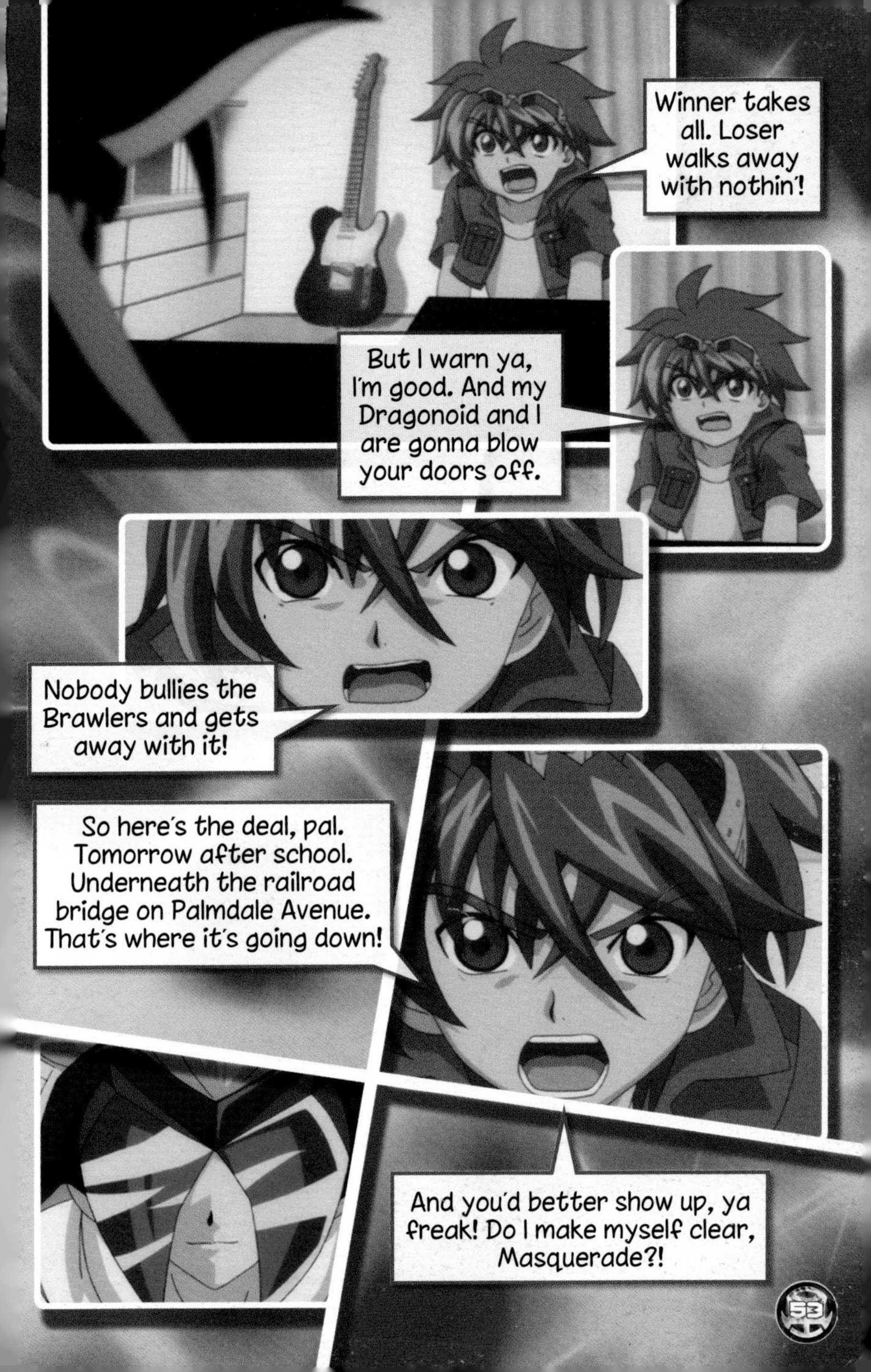

Winner takes all. Loser walks away with nothin'!
But I warn ya, I'm good. And my Dragonoid and I are gonna blow your doors off.
Nobody bullies the Brawlers and gets away with it!
So here's the deal, pal. Tomorrow after school. Underneath the railroad bridge on Palmdale Avenue. That's where it's going down!
And you'd better show up, ya freak! Do I make myself clear, Masquerade?!

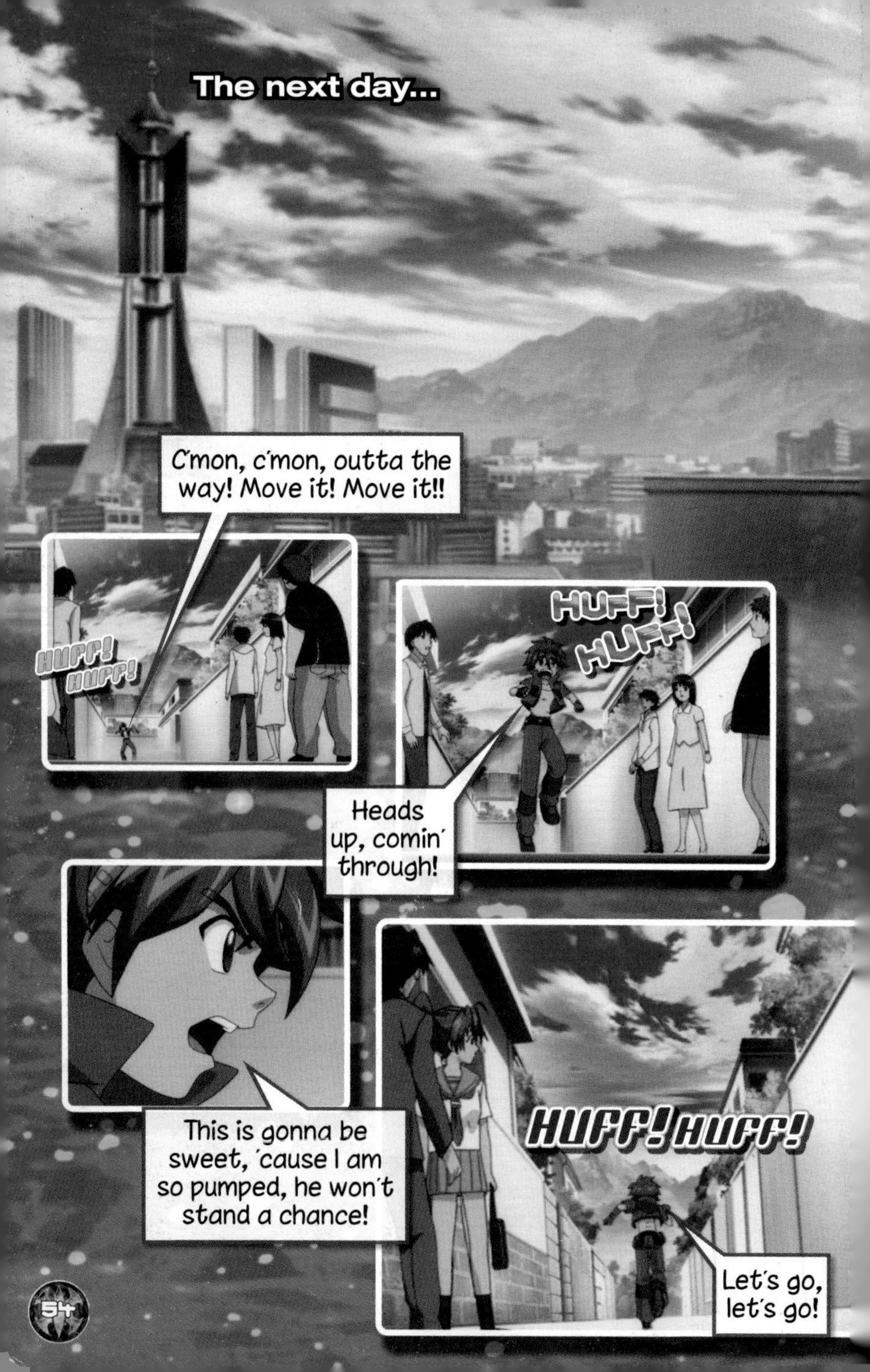
The next day...
C'mon, c'mon, outta the way! Move it! Move it!!
HUFF! HUFF!
HUFF! HUFF!
Heads up, comin' through!
This is gonna be sweet, 'cause I am so pumped, he won't stand a chance!
HUFF! HUFF!
Let's go, let's go!

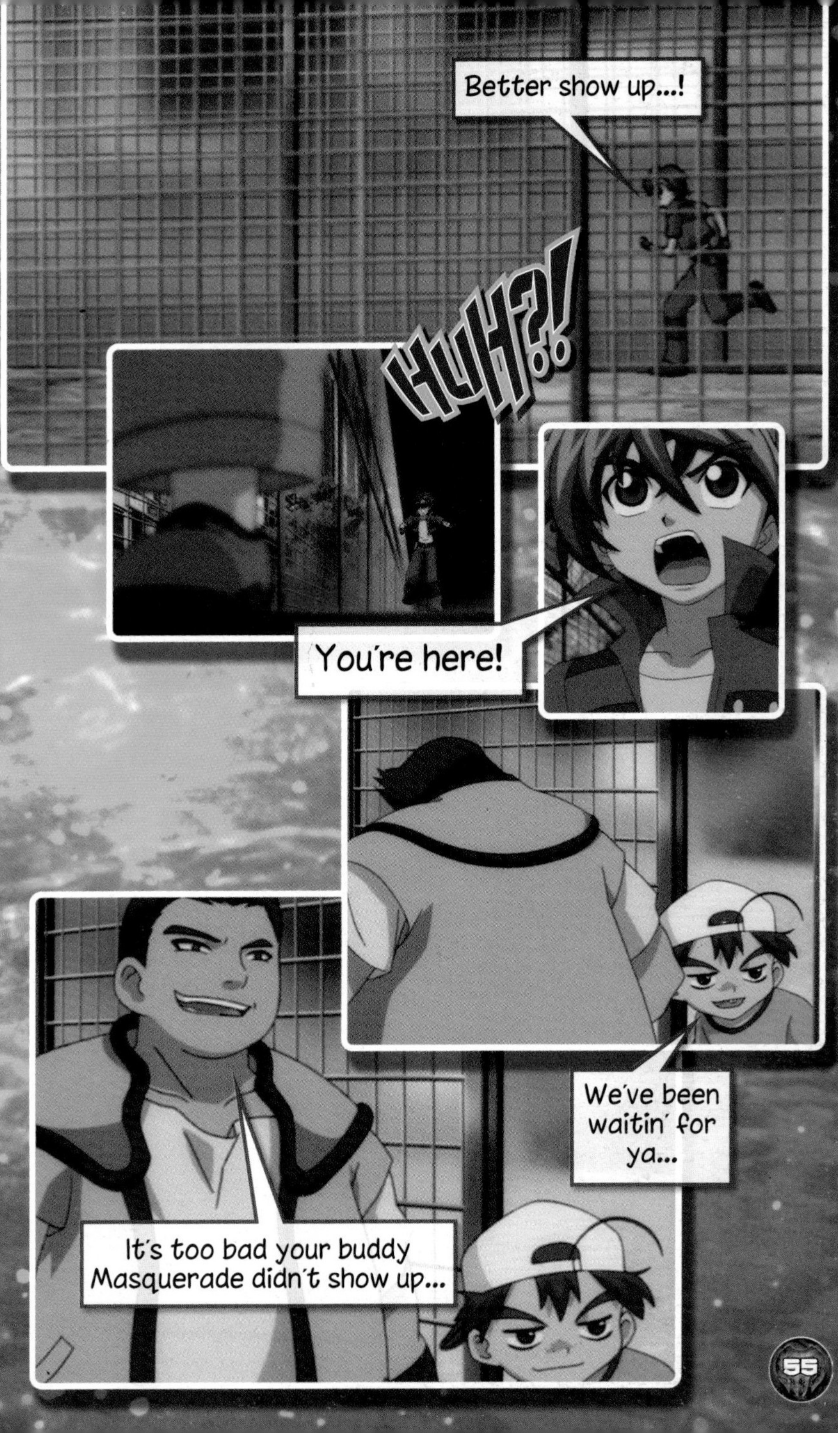
Better show up...!
HUH?!
You're here!
We've been waitin' for ya...
It's too bad your buddy Masquerade didn't show up...

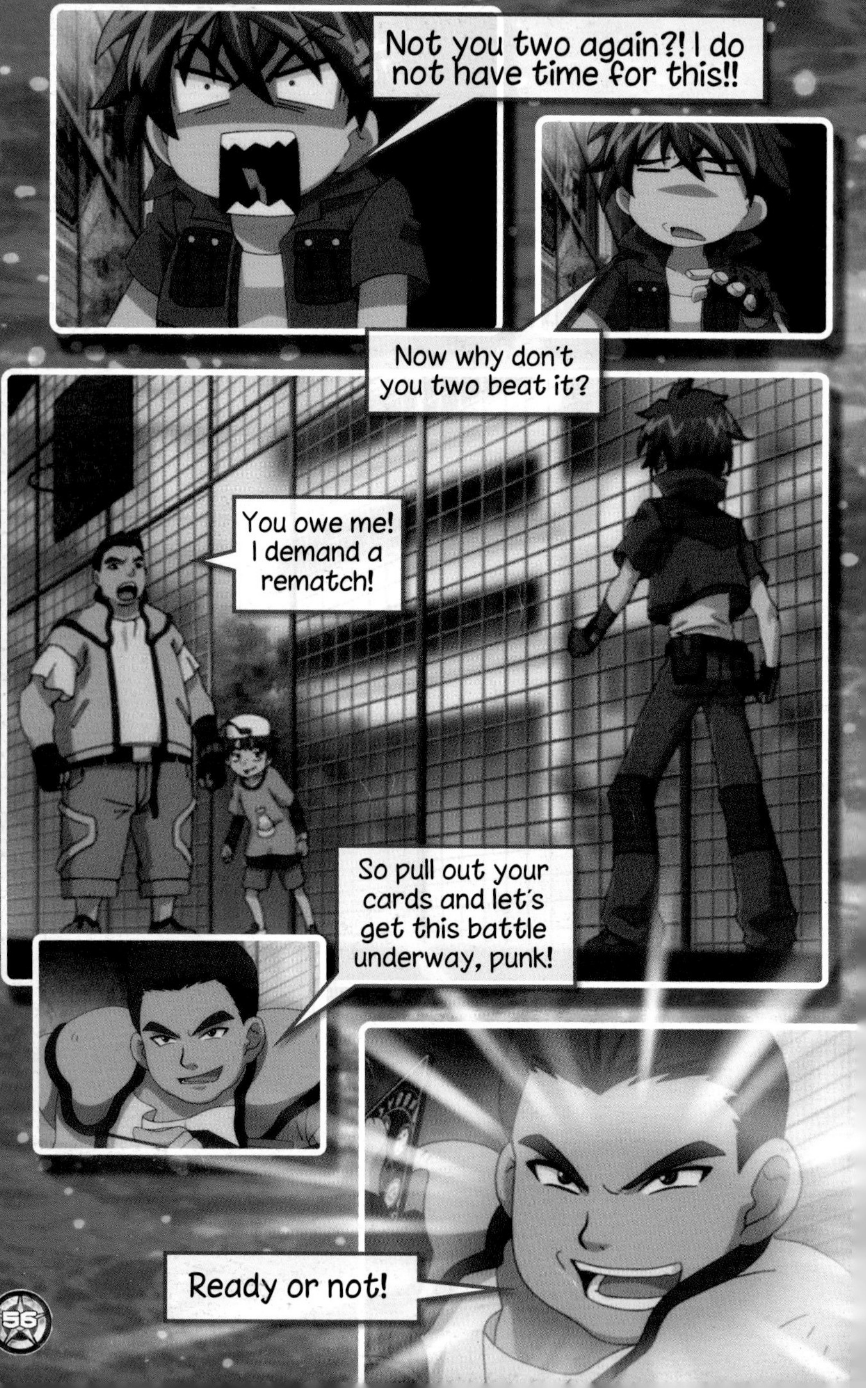
Not you two again?! I do not have time for this!!
Now why don't you two beat it?
You owe me! I demand a rematch!
So pull out your cards and let's get this battle underway, punk!
Ready or not!

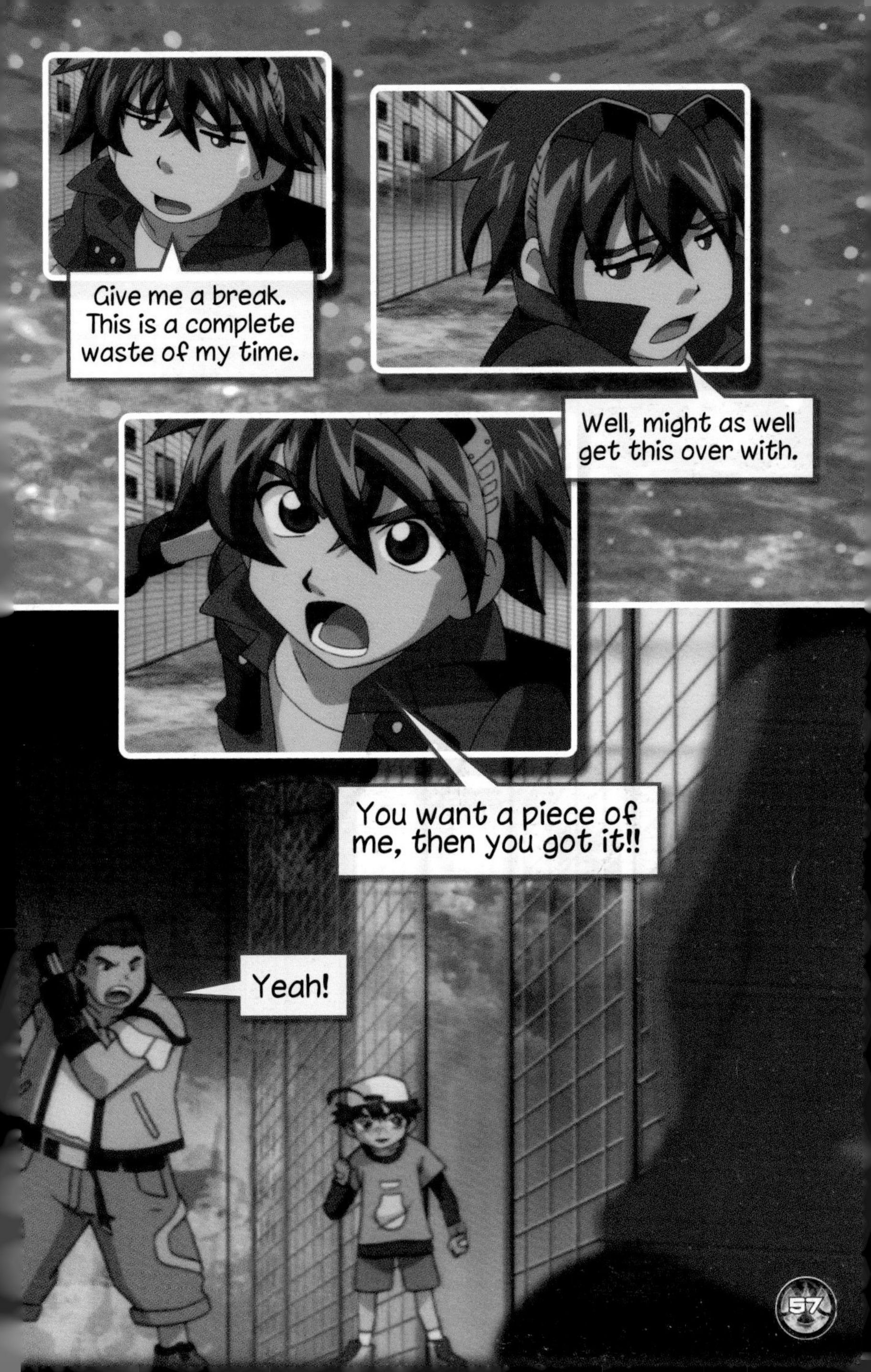
Give me a break. This is a complete waste of my time.
Well, might as well get this over with.
You want a piece of me, then you got it!!
Yeah!

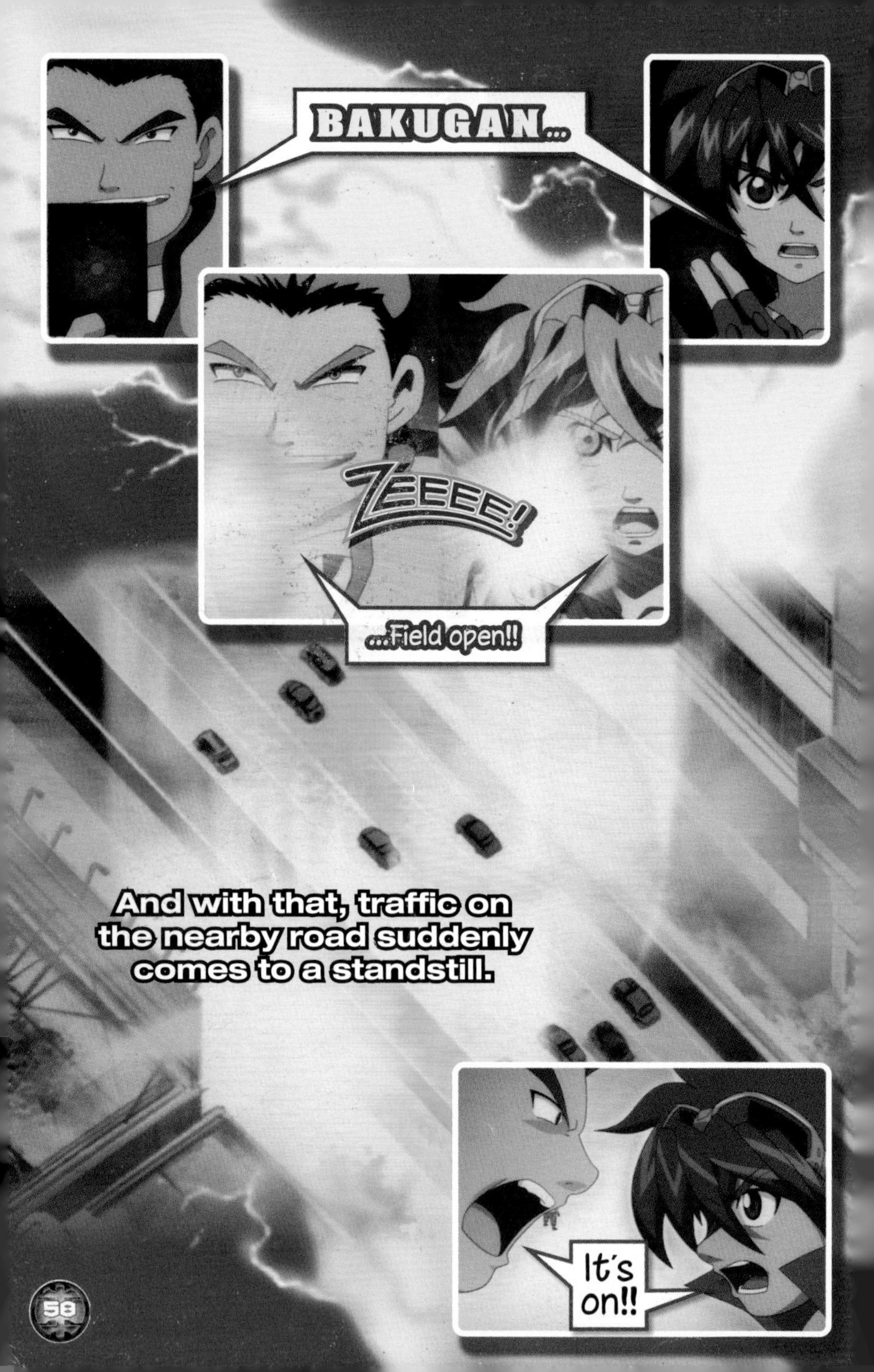
BAKUGAN...
ZEEEEE!
...Field open!!
And with that, traffic on the nearby road suddenly comes to a standstill.
It's on!!

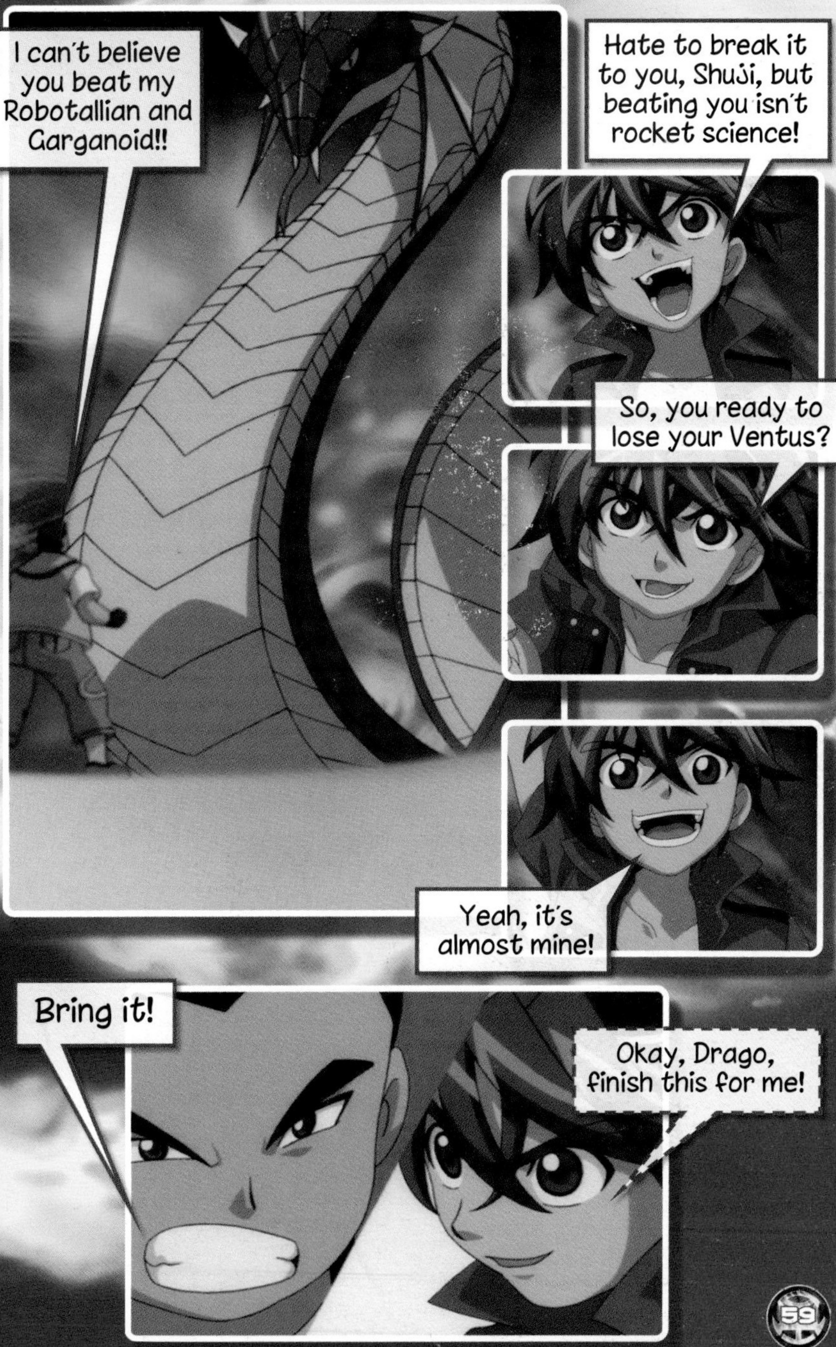
I can't believe you beat my Robotallian and Garganoid!!
Hate to break it to you, Shuji, but beating you isn't rocket science!
So, you ready to lose your Ventus?
Yeah, it's almost mine!
Bring it!
Okay, Drago, finish this for me!

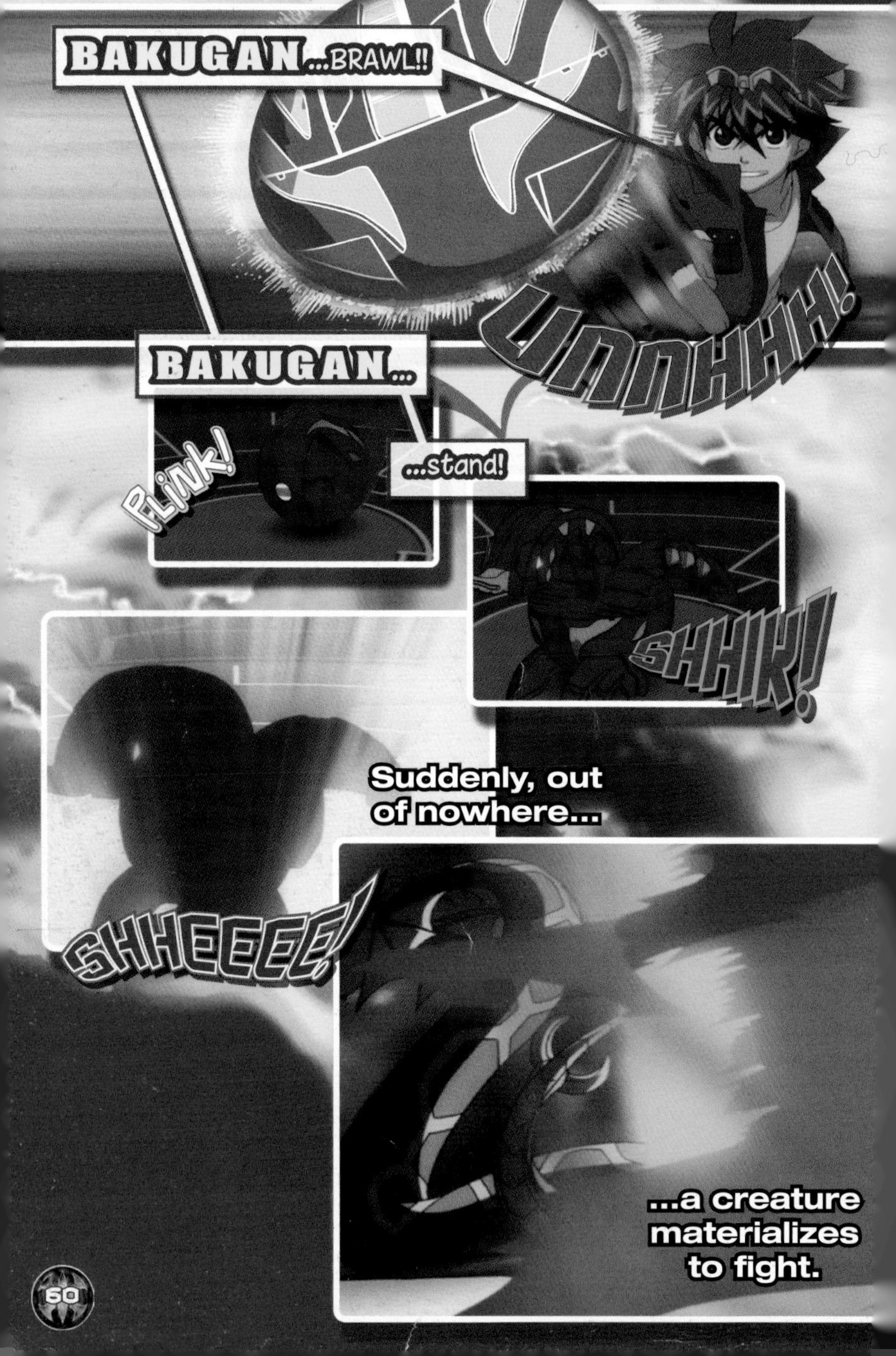
BAKUGAN...BRAWL!!
UNNHHH!
BAKUGAN...
PLINK!
...stand!
SHHK!
Suddenly, out of nowhere...
SHHEEEE!
...a creature materializes to fight.

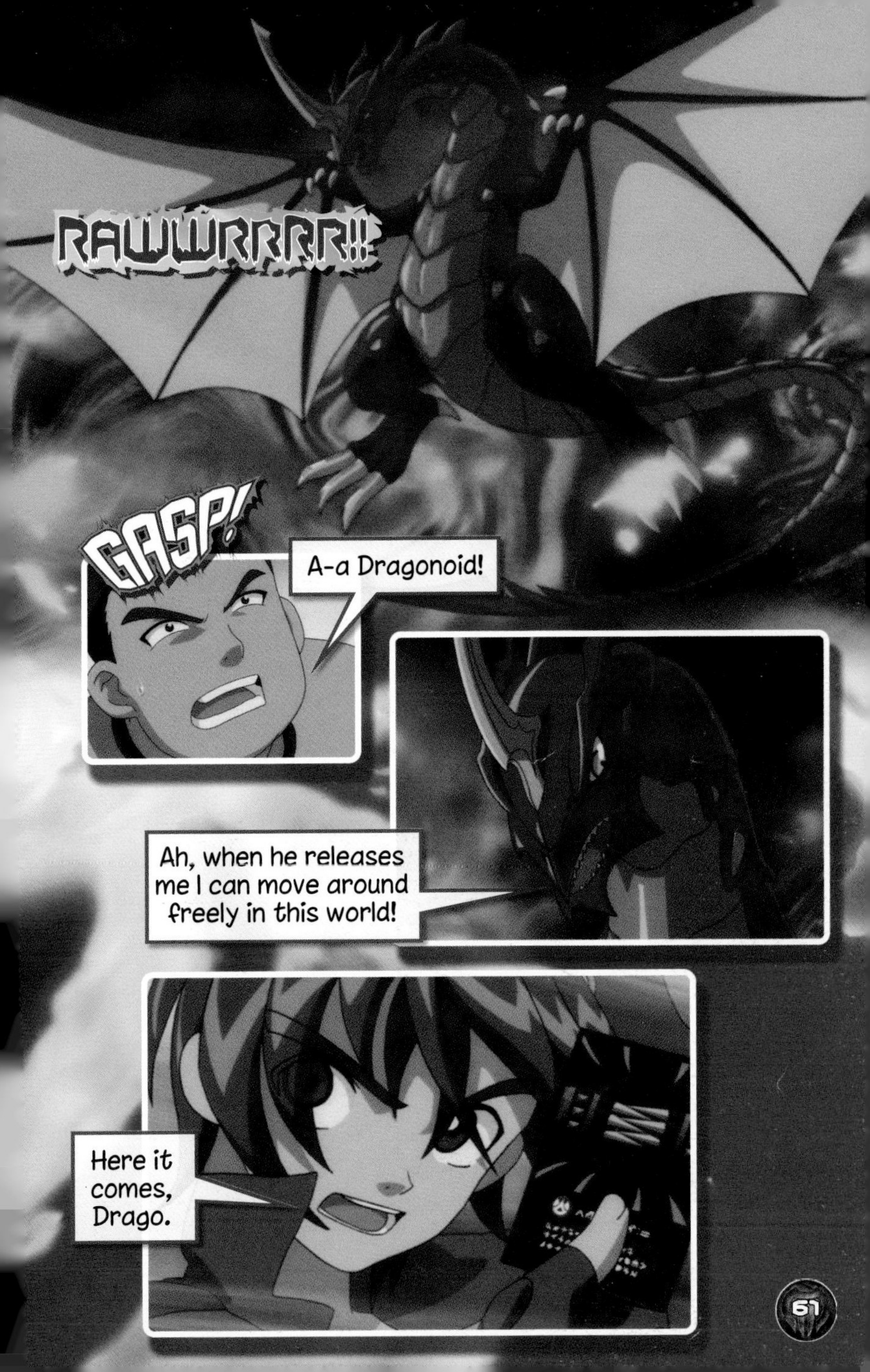
RAWWRRRR!!
GASP!
A-a Dragonoid!
Ah, when he releases me I can move around freely in this world!
Here it comes, Drago.

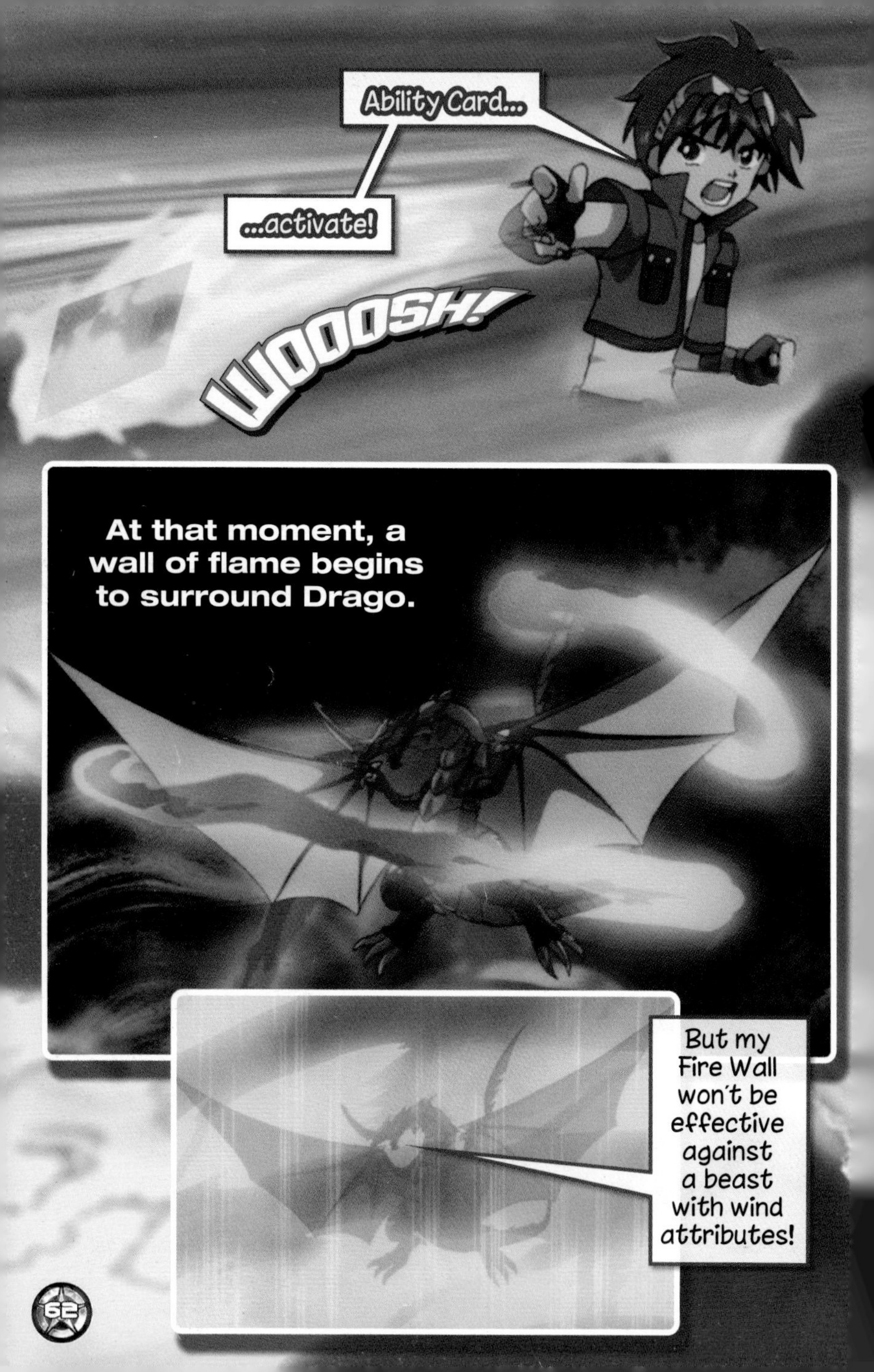
Ability Card...
...activate!
WOOOSH!
At that moment, a wall of flame begins to surround Drago.
But my Fire Wall won't be effective against a beast with wind attributes!

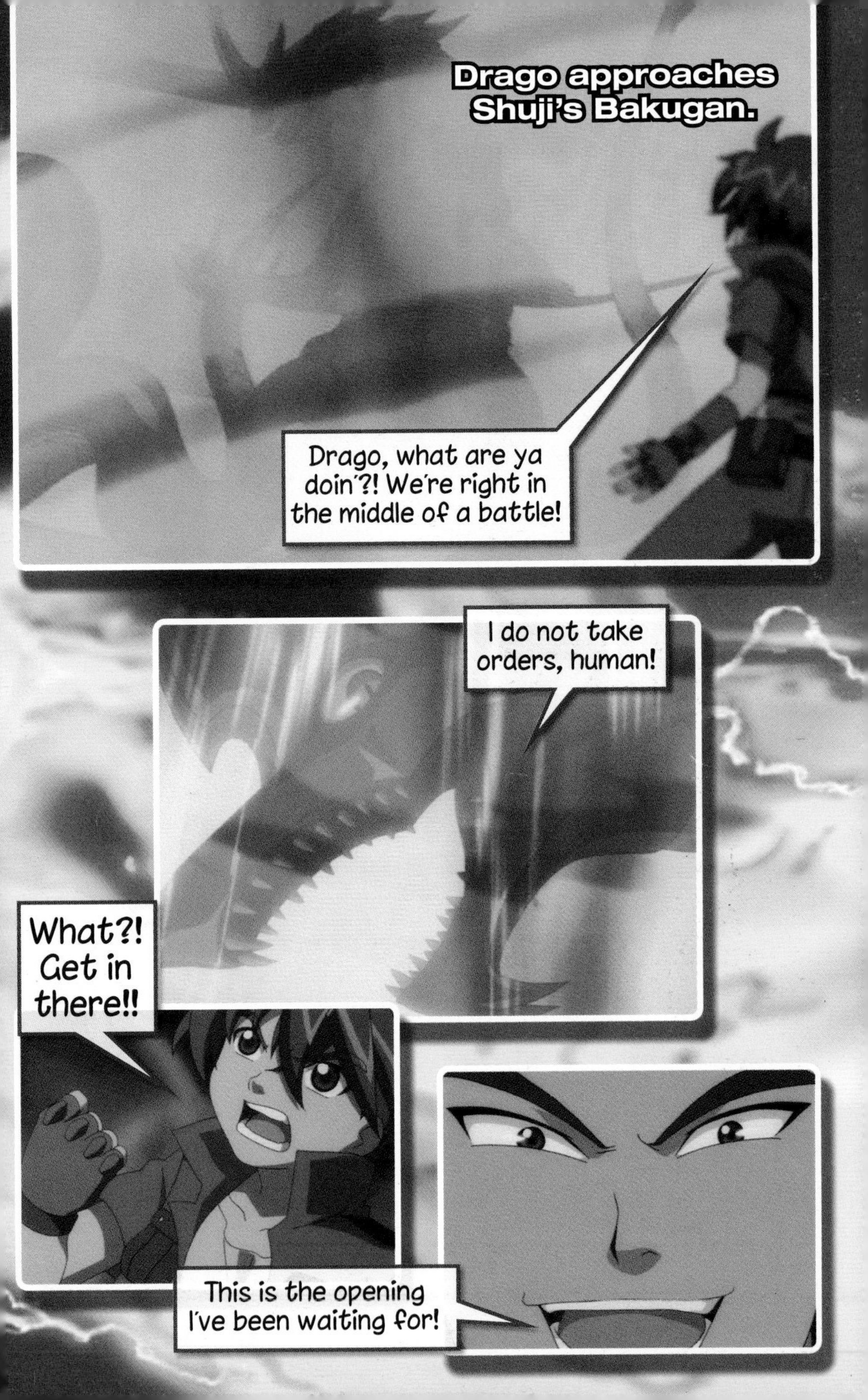
Drago approaches Shuji's Bakugan.
Drago, what are ya doin'?! We're right in the middle of a battle!
I do not take orders, human!
What?! Get in there!!
This is the opening I've been waiting for!

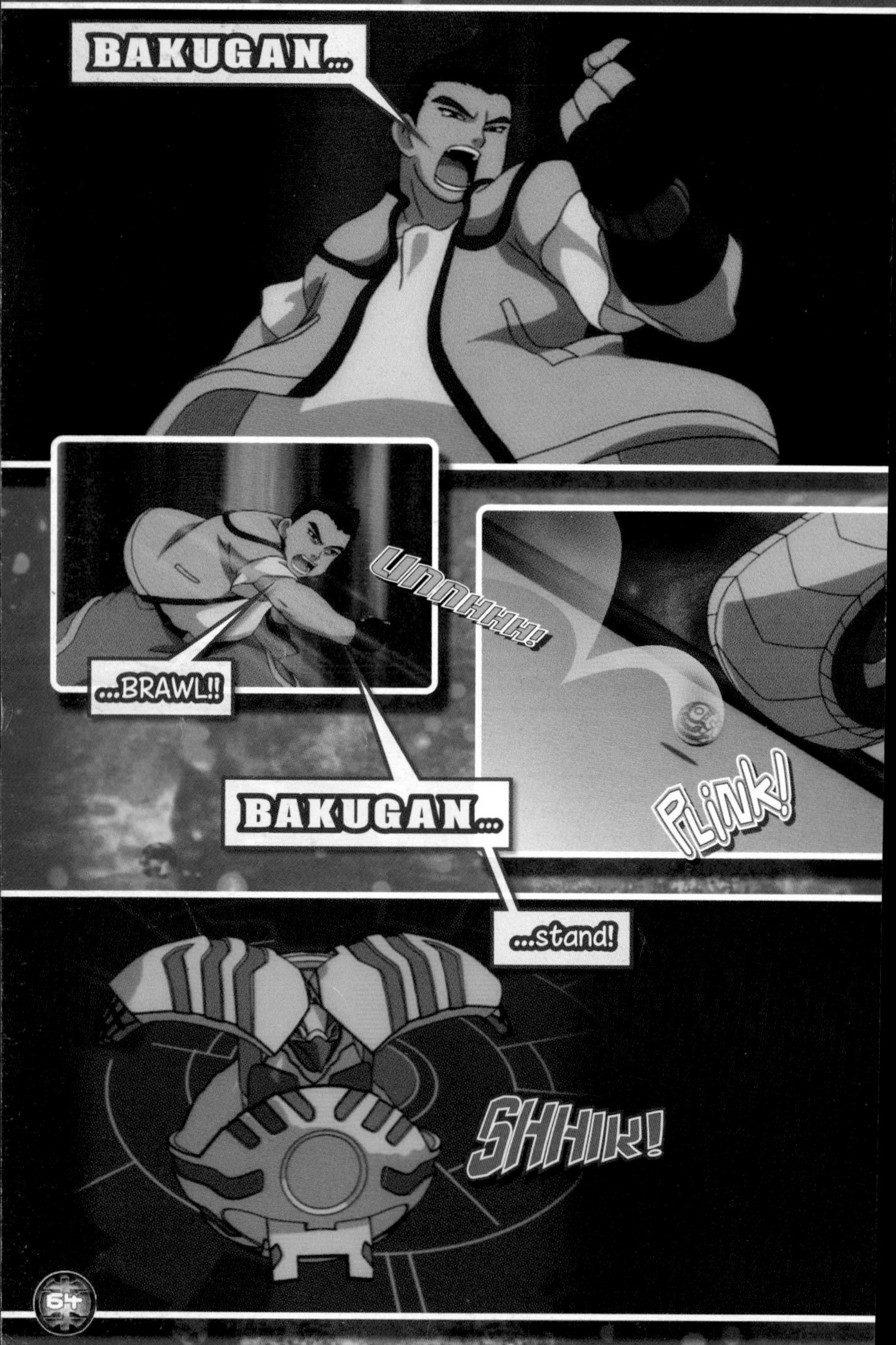
BAKUGAN...
...BRAWL!!
UNNHHH!
PLINK!
BAKUGAN...
...stand!
SHHIK!

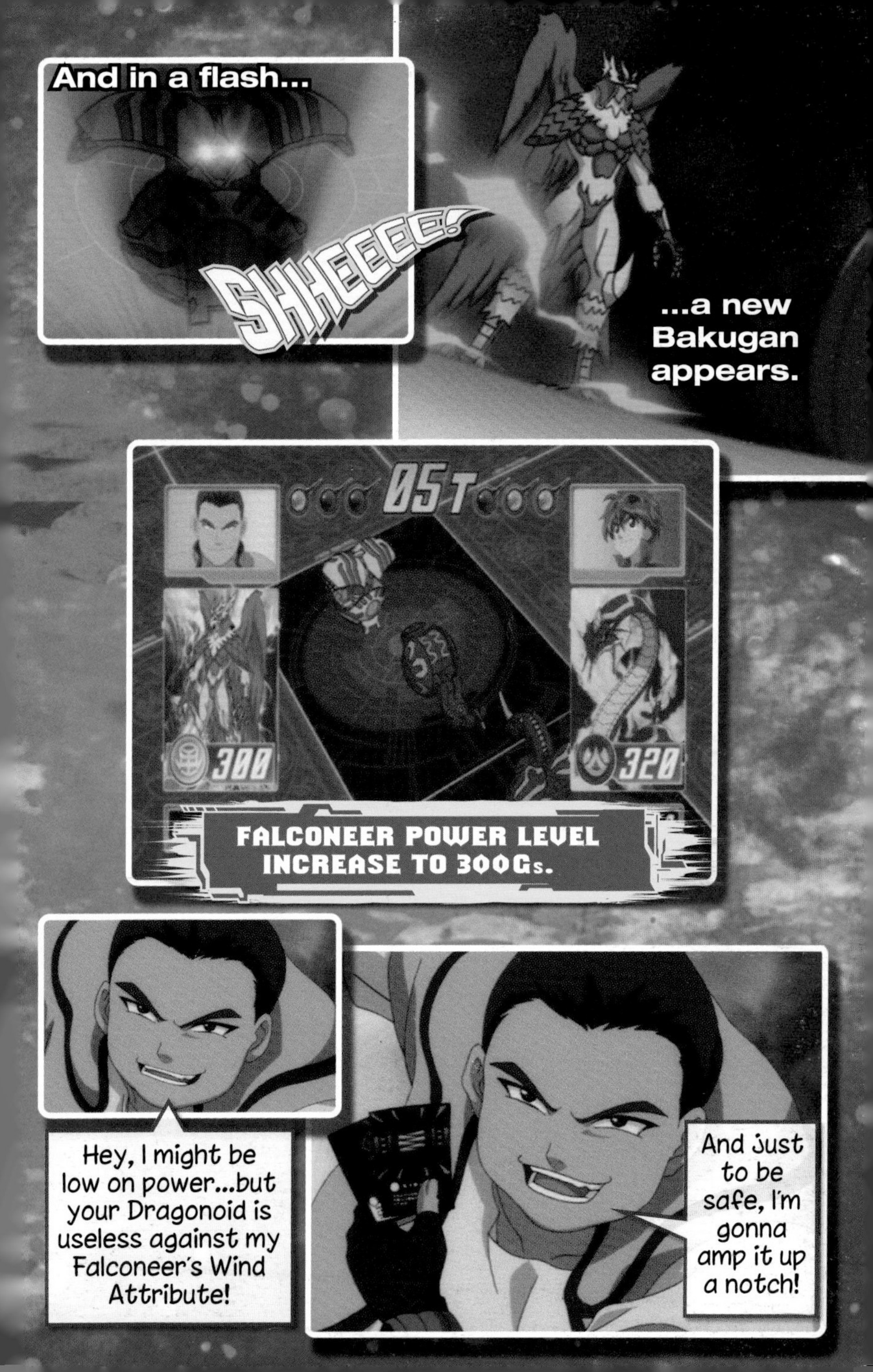
And in a flash...
SHHEEEEE!
...a new Bakugan appears.
05 T
300
320
FALCONEER POWER LEVEL INCREASE TO 300Gs.
Hey, I might be low on power...but your Dragonoid is useless against my Falconeer's Wind Attribute!
And just to be safe, I'm gonna amp it up a notch!

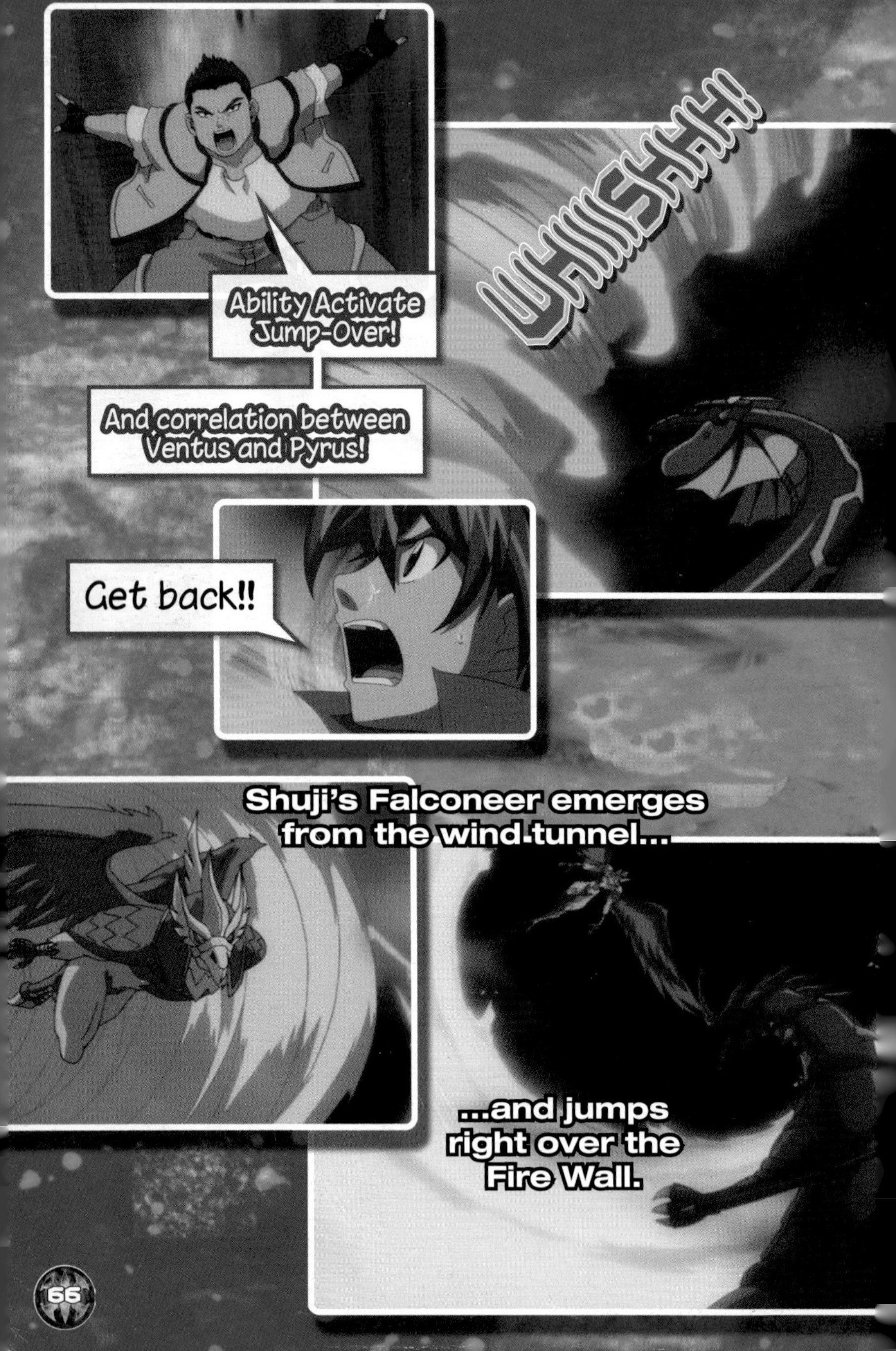
Ability Activate Jump-Over!
And correlation between Ventus and Pyrus!
Get back!!
Shuji's Falconeer emerges from the wind tunnel...
...and jumps right over the Fire Wall.

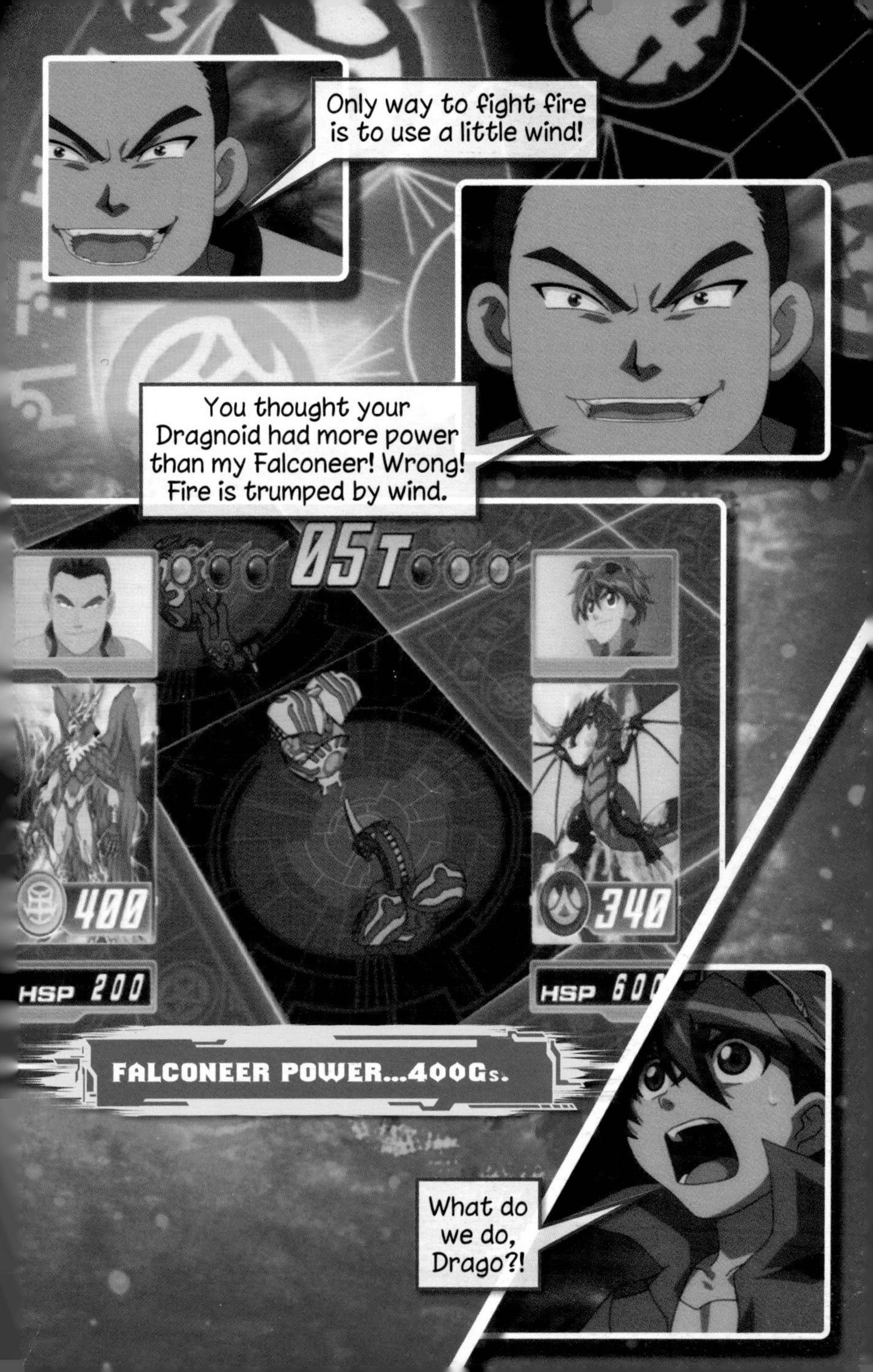

Only way to fight fire is to use a little wind!
You thought your Dragnoid had more power than my Falconeer! Wrong! Fire is trumped by wind.
05T
400
HSP 200
340
HSP 600
FALCONEER POWER...400Gs.
What do we do, Drago?!

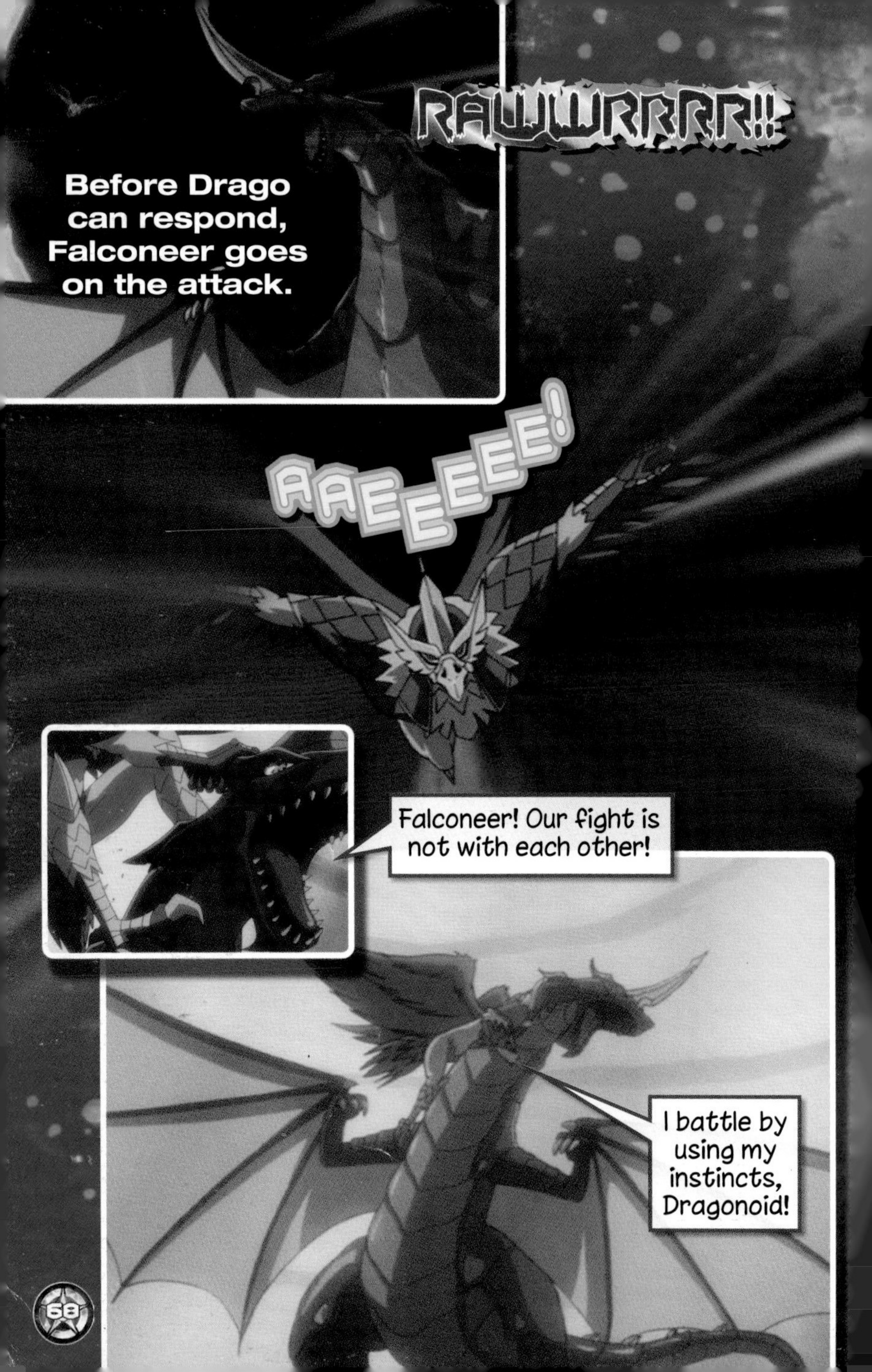
Before Drago can respond, Falconeer goes on the attack.
RAWWRRRR!!
AAEEEEE!
Falconeer! Our fight is not with each other!
I battle by using my instincts, Dragonoid!

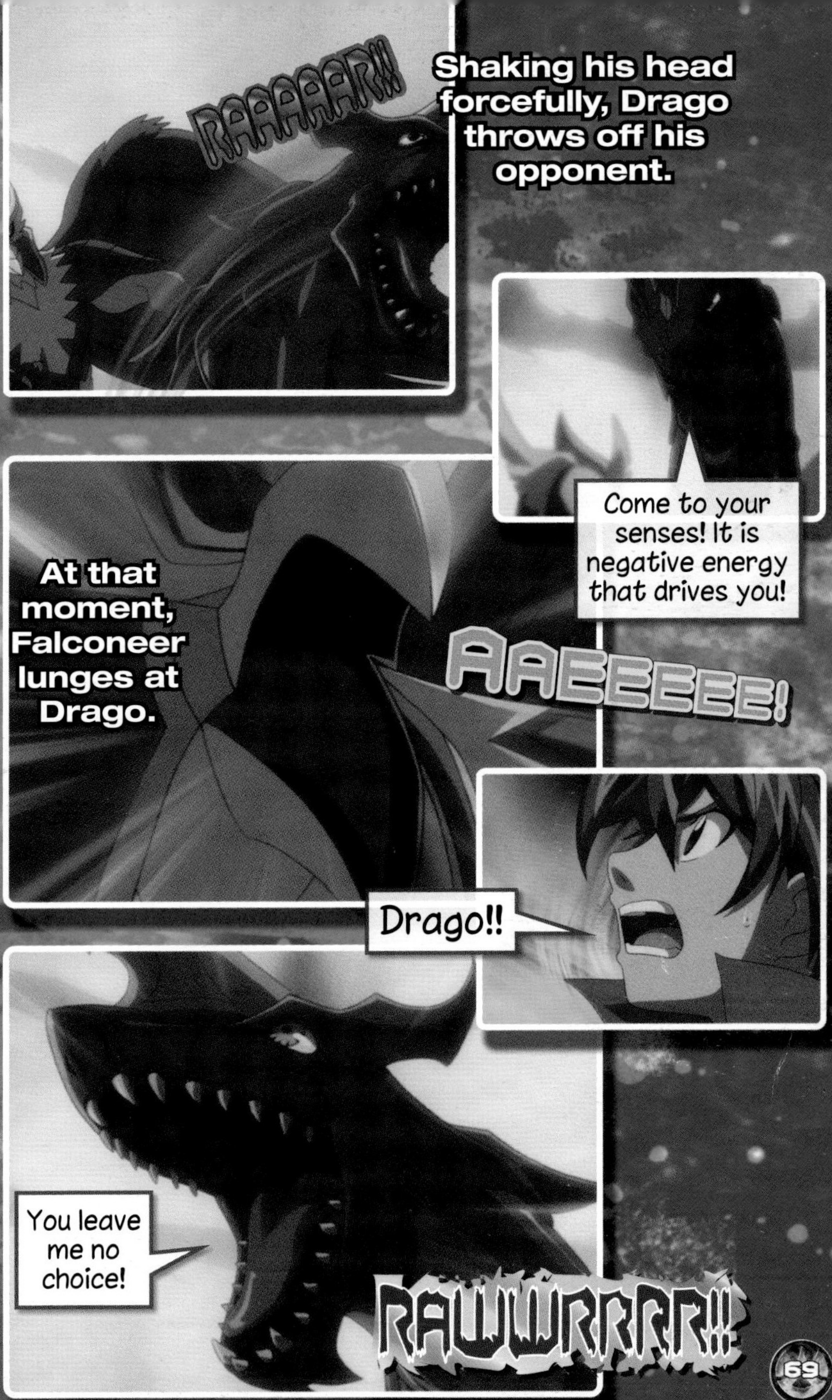
RAAAAAAR!!
Shaking his head forcefully, Drago throws off his opponent.
Come to your senses! It is negative energy that drives you!
At that moment, Falconeer lunges at Drago.
AAEEEEEE!
Drago!!
You leave me no choice!
RAWWRRRR!!

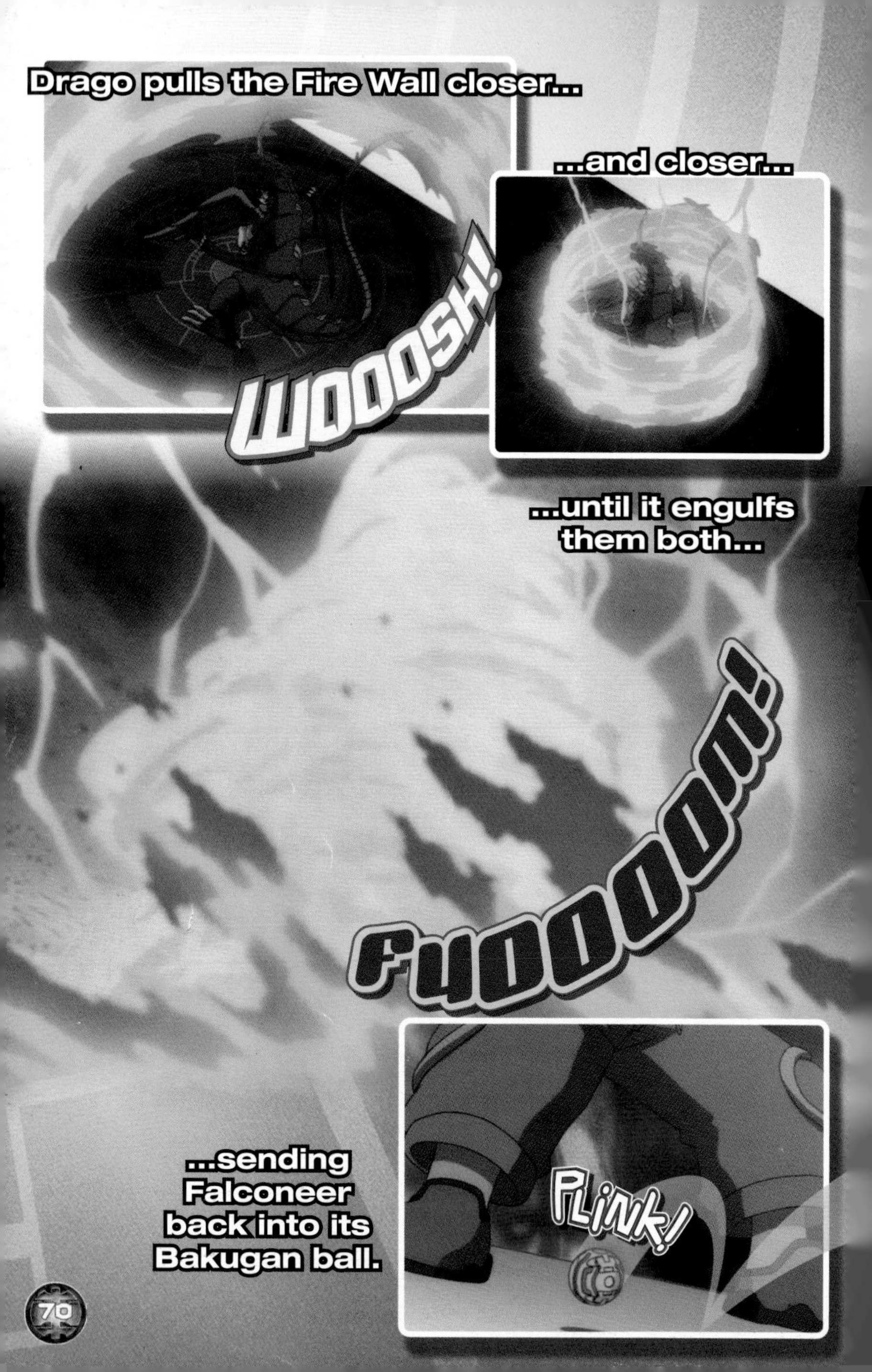

Drago pulls the Fire Wall closer...

WOOOSH!

...and closer...

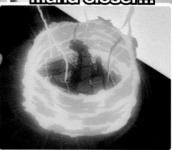

...until it engulfs them both...

FWOOOOM!

...sending Falconeer back into its Bakugan ball.

PLINK!

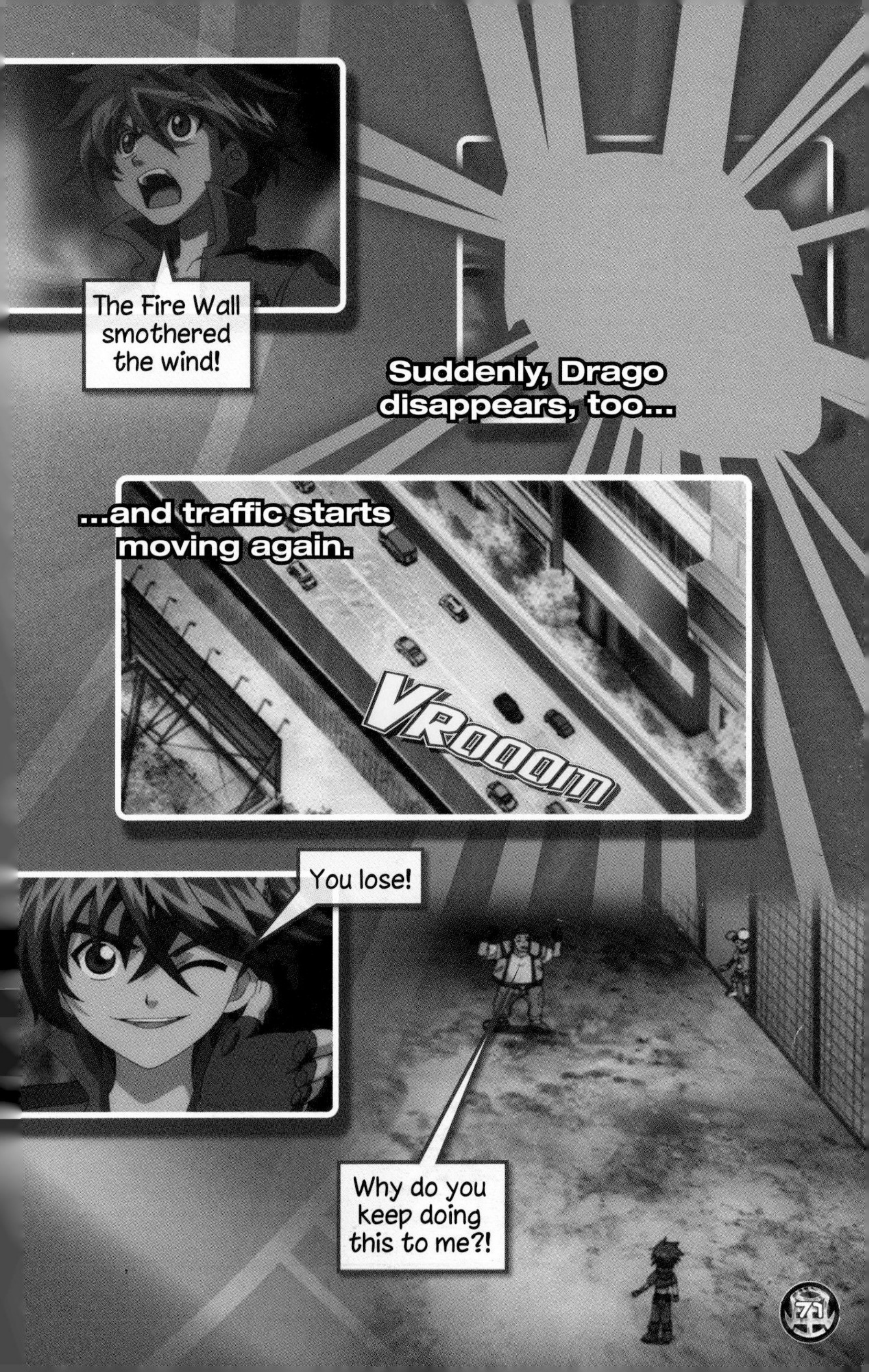

The Fire Wall smothered the wind!
Suddenly, Drago disappears, too...
...and traffic starts moving again.
VROOOM
You lose!
Why do you keep doing this to me?!

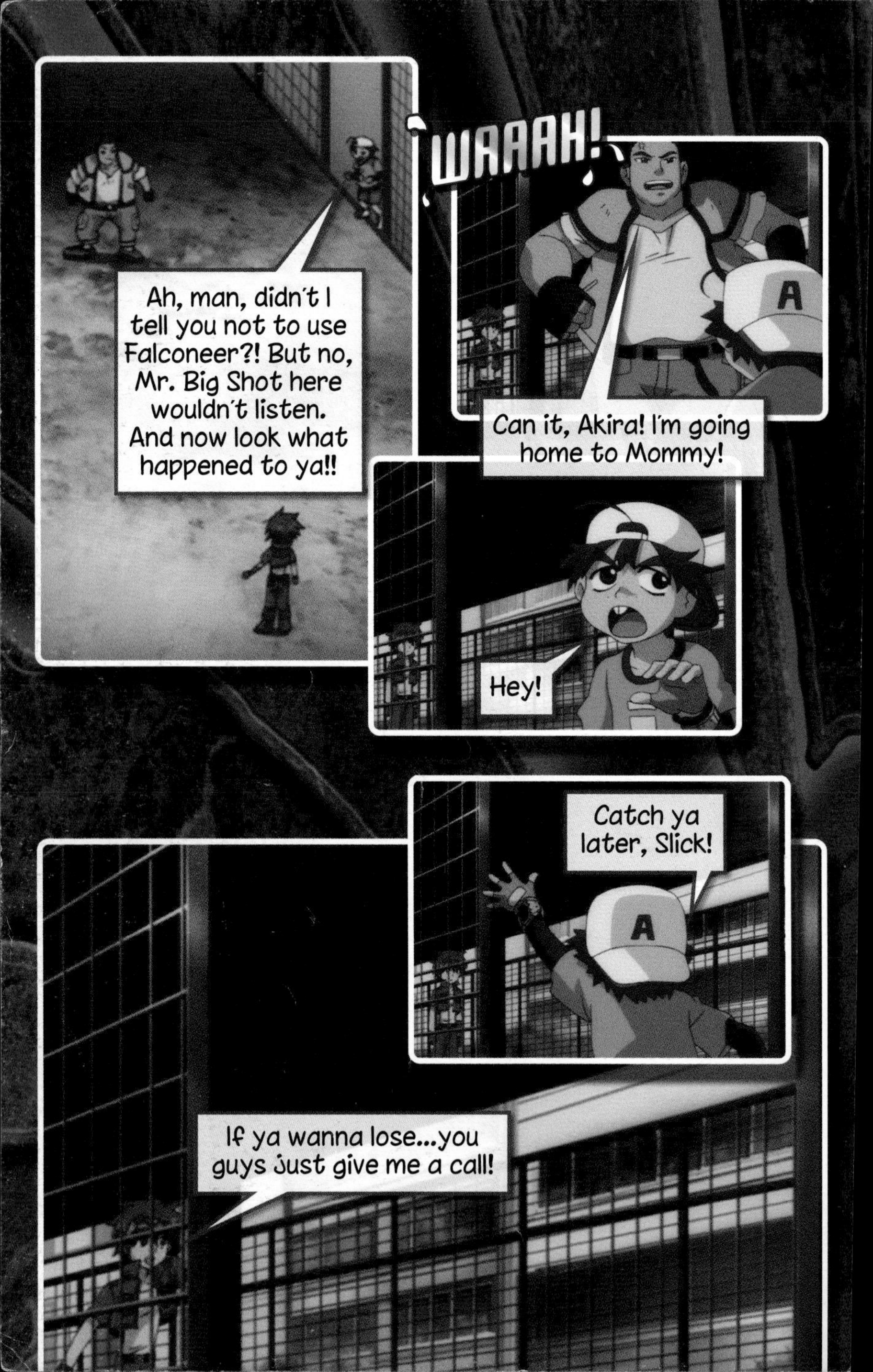
Ah, man, didn't I tell you not to use Falconeer?! But no, Mr. Big Shot here wouldn't listen. And now look what happened to ya!!
WAAAH!
Can it, Akira! I'm going home to Mommy!
Hey!
Catch ya later, Slick!
If ya wanna lose...you guys just give me a call!

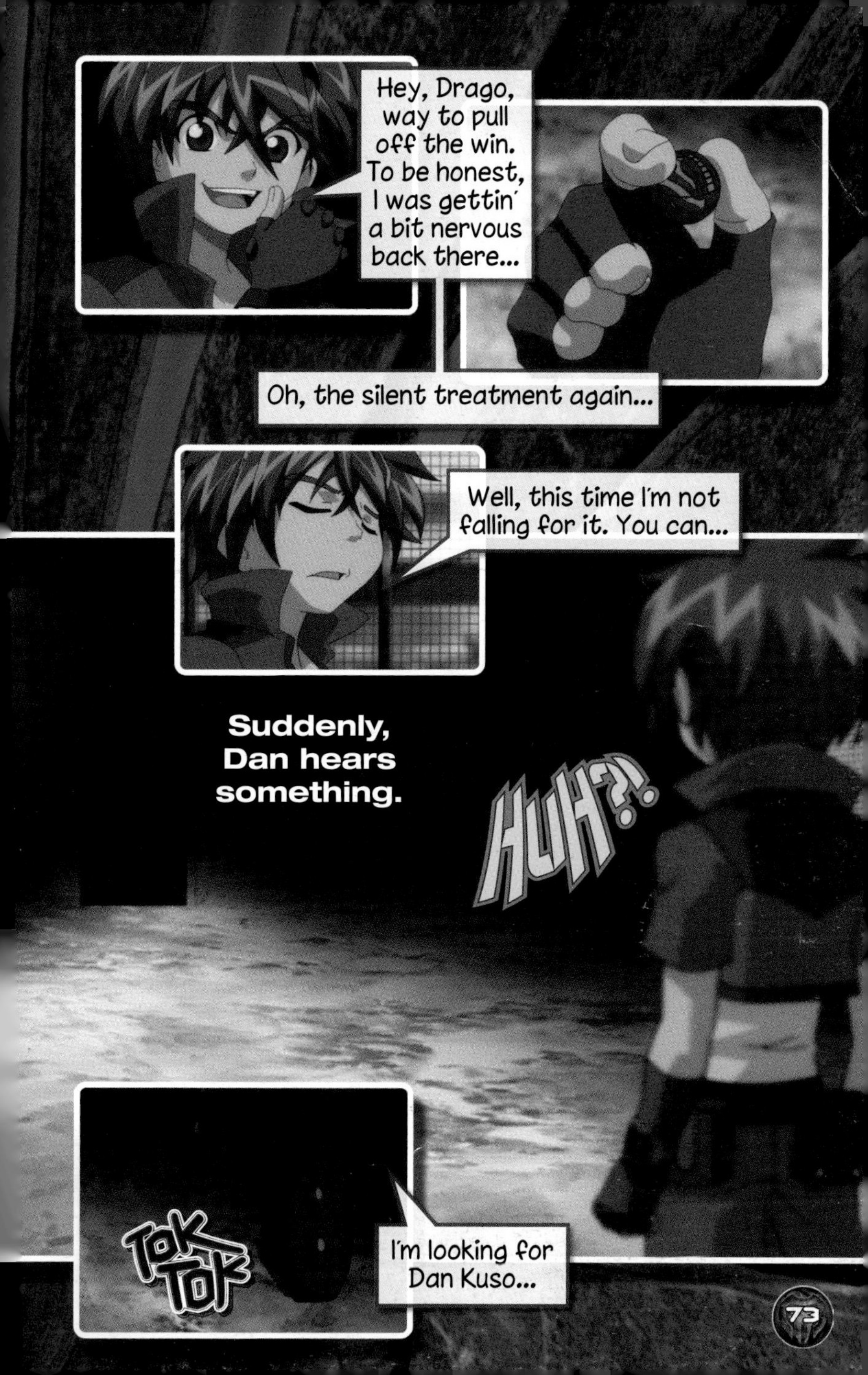
Hey, Drago, way to pull off the win. To be honest, I was gettin' a bit nervous back there...
Oh, the silent treatment again...
Well, this time I'm not falling for it. You can...
Suddenly, Dan hears something.
HUH?!
TOK TOK
I'm looking for Dan Kuso...

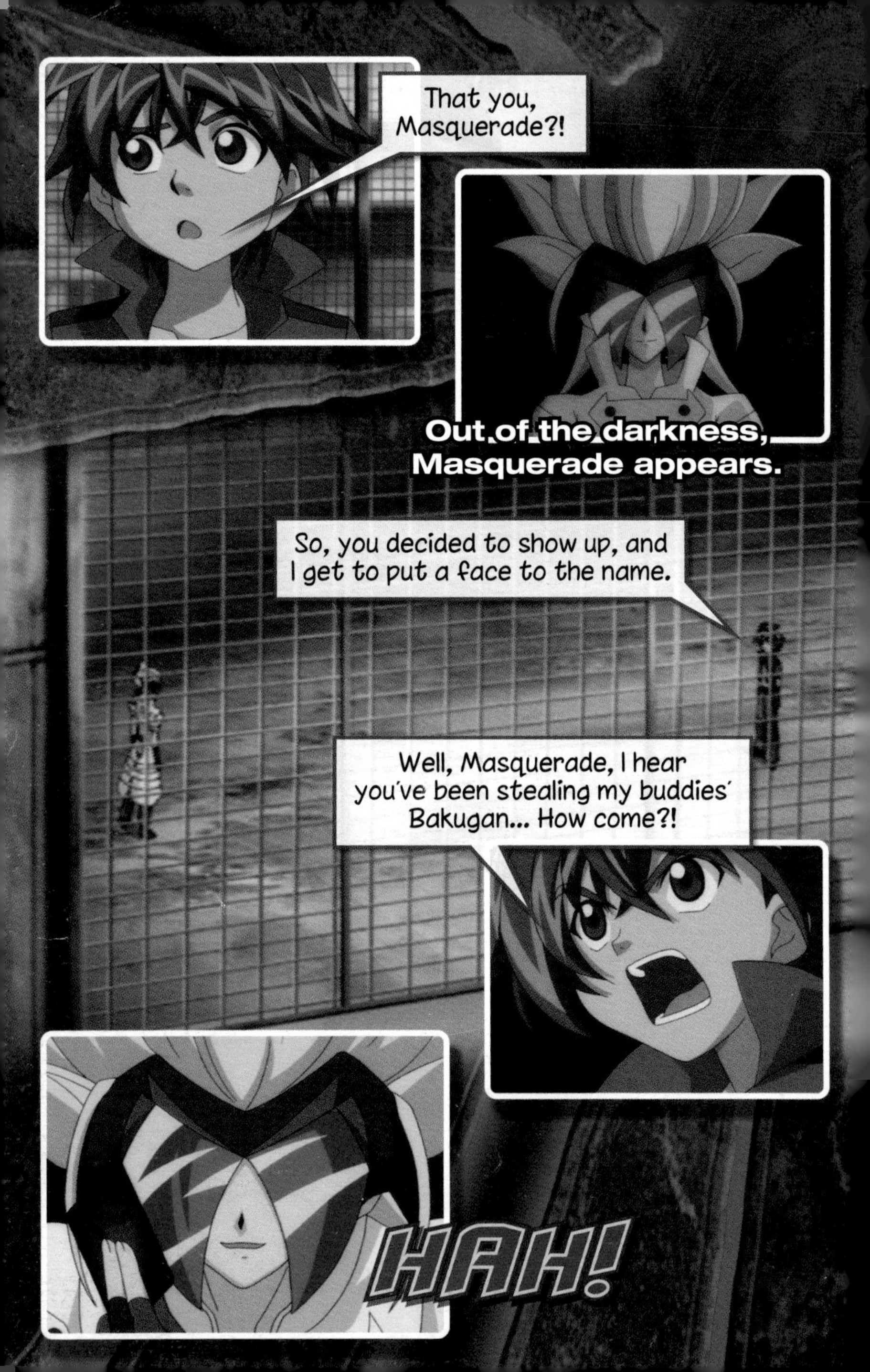
That you, Masquerade?!
Out of the darkness, Masquerade appears.
So, you decided to show up, and I get to put a face to the name.
Well, Masquerade, I hear you've been stealing my buddies' Bakugan... How come?!
HAH!

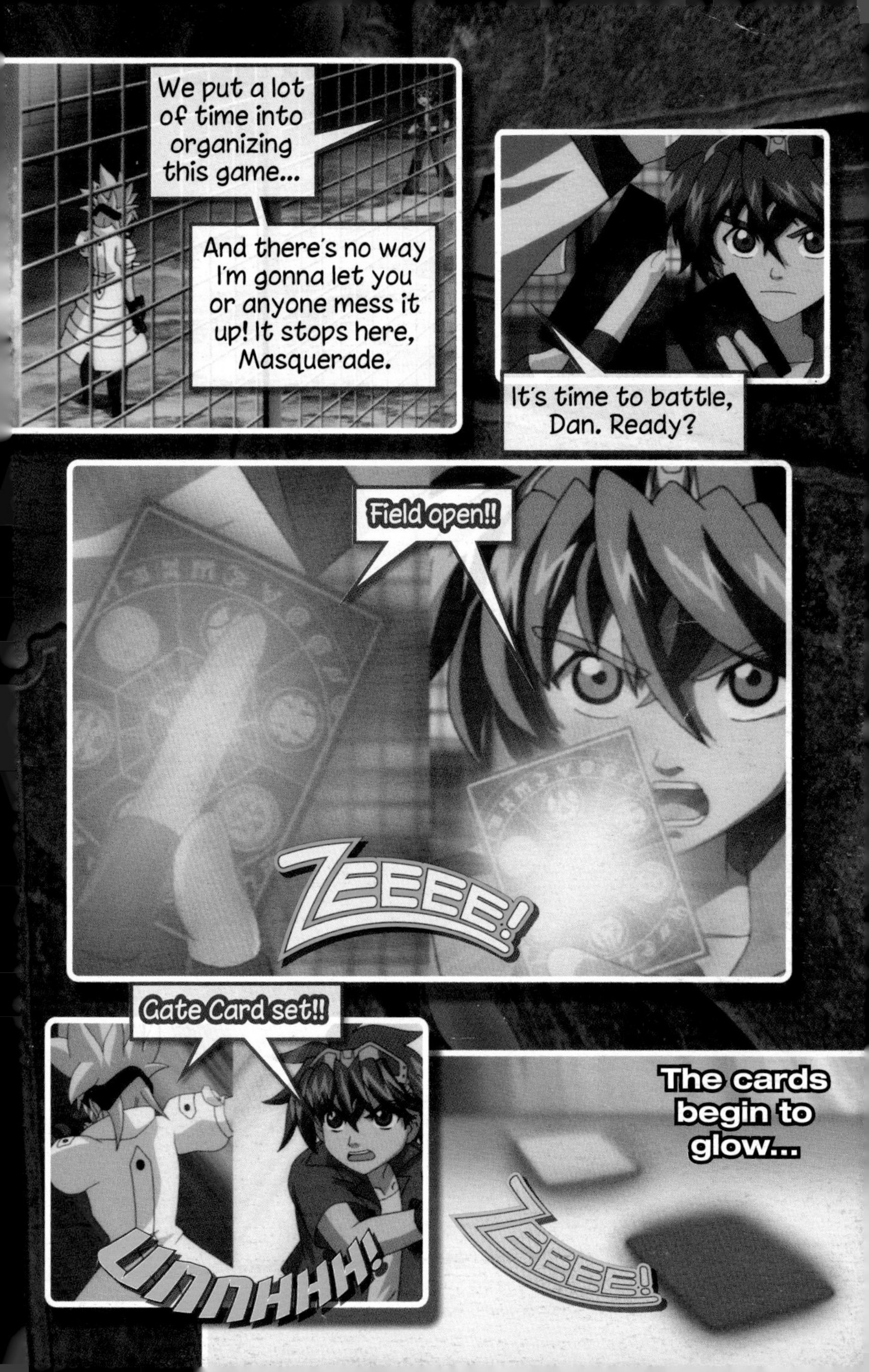
We put a lot of time into organizing this game...
And there's no way I'm gonna let you or anyone mess it up! It stops here, Masquerade.
It's time to battle, Dan. Ready?
Field open!!
ZEEEE!
Gate Card set!!
UNNHHH!
The cards begin to glow...
ZEEEE!

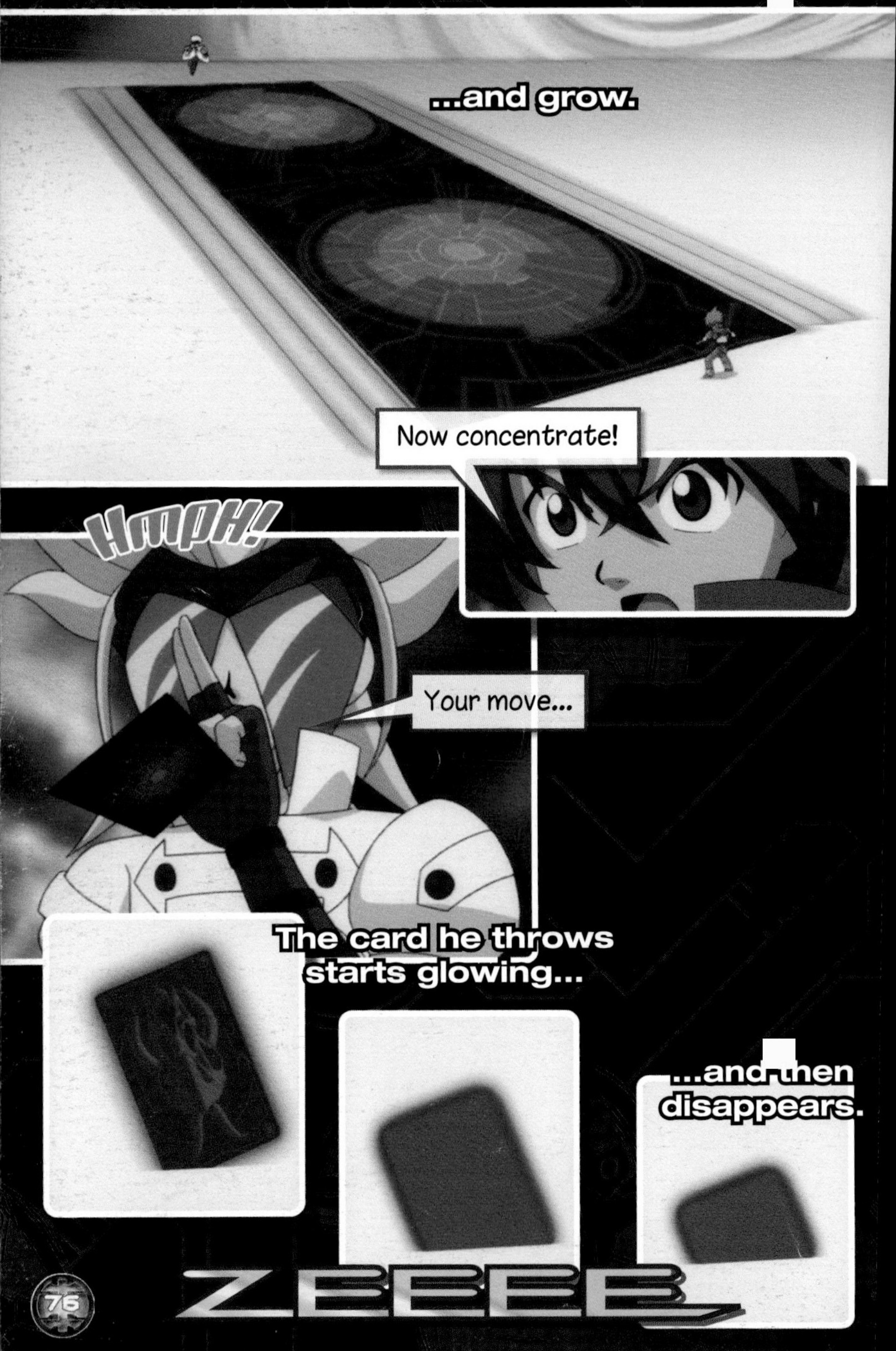
...and grow.
Now concentrate!
HMPH!
Your move...
The card he throws starts glowing...
...and then disappears.
ZEEEE

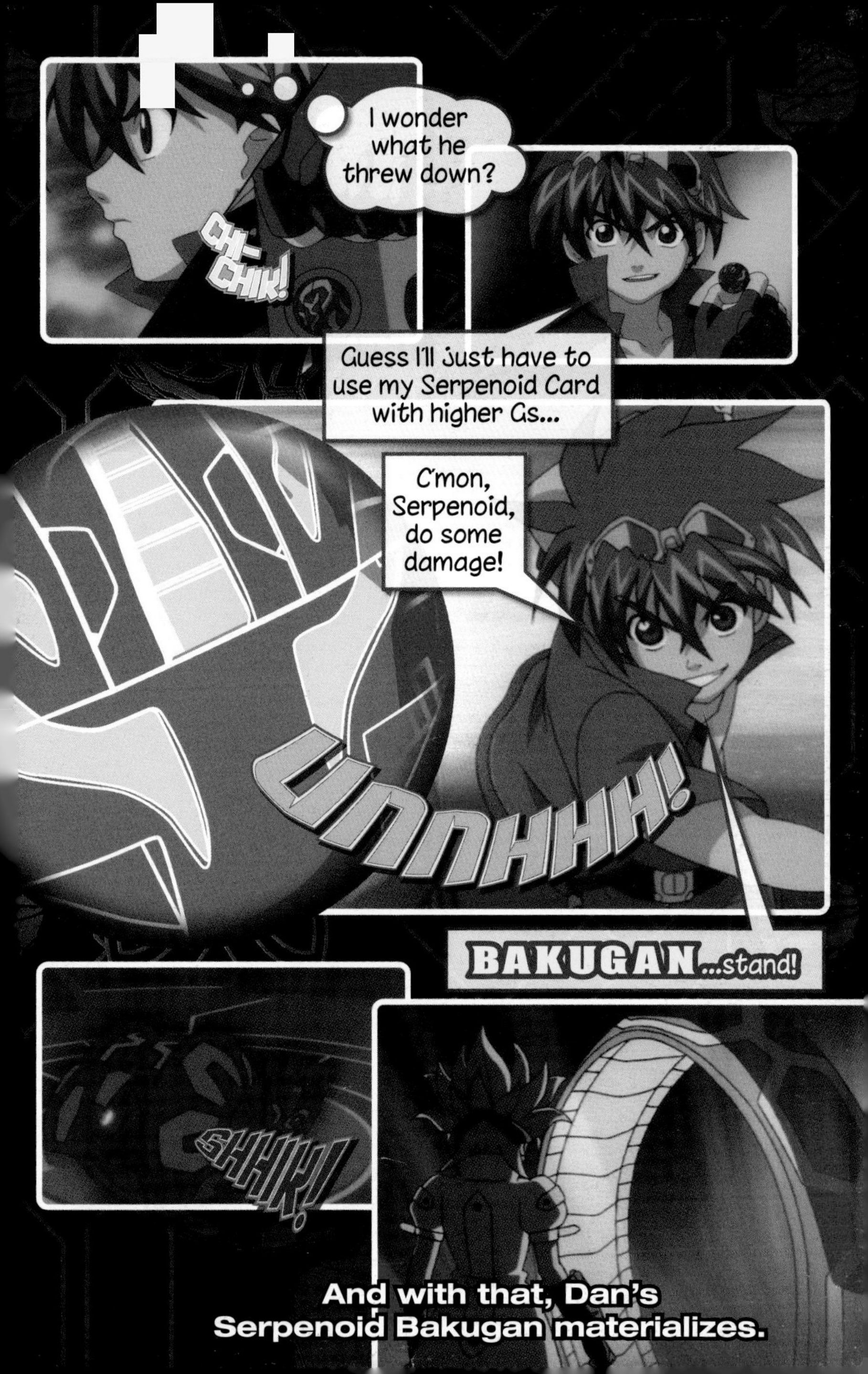

I wonder what he threw down?
CHI-CHIK!
Guess I'll just have to use my Serpenoid Card with higher Gs...
C'mon, Serpenoid, do some damage!
UNNHHH!
BAKUGAN...stand!
SHHIK!
And with that, Dan's Serpenoid Bakugan materializes.

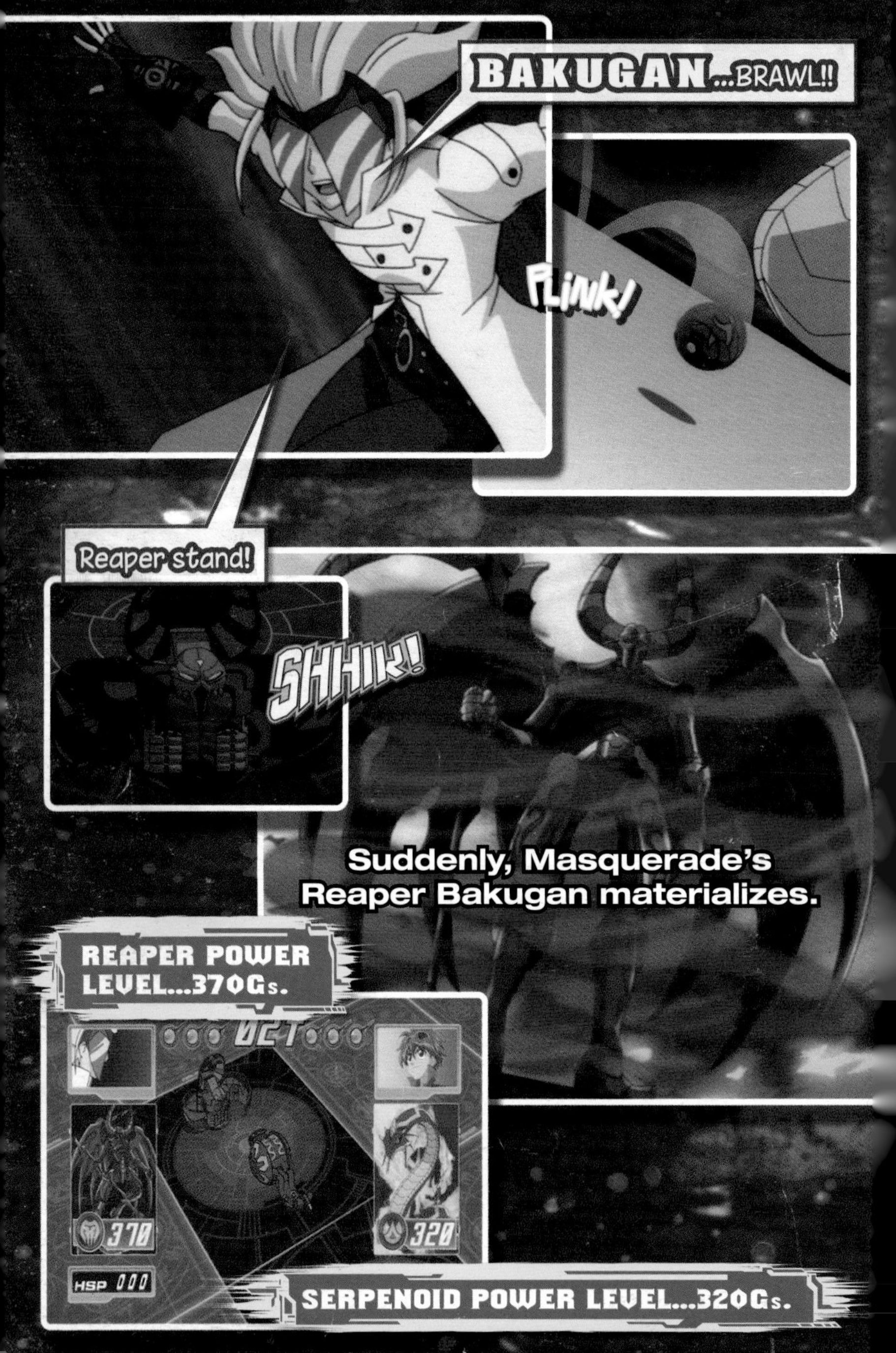
BAKUGAN...BRAWL!!
PLINK!
Reaper stand!
SHHIK!
Suddenly, Masquerade's Reaper Bakugan materializes.
REAPER POWER LEVEL...370Gs.
370
320
HSP 000
SERPENOID POWER LEVEL...320Gs.

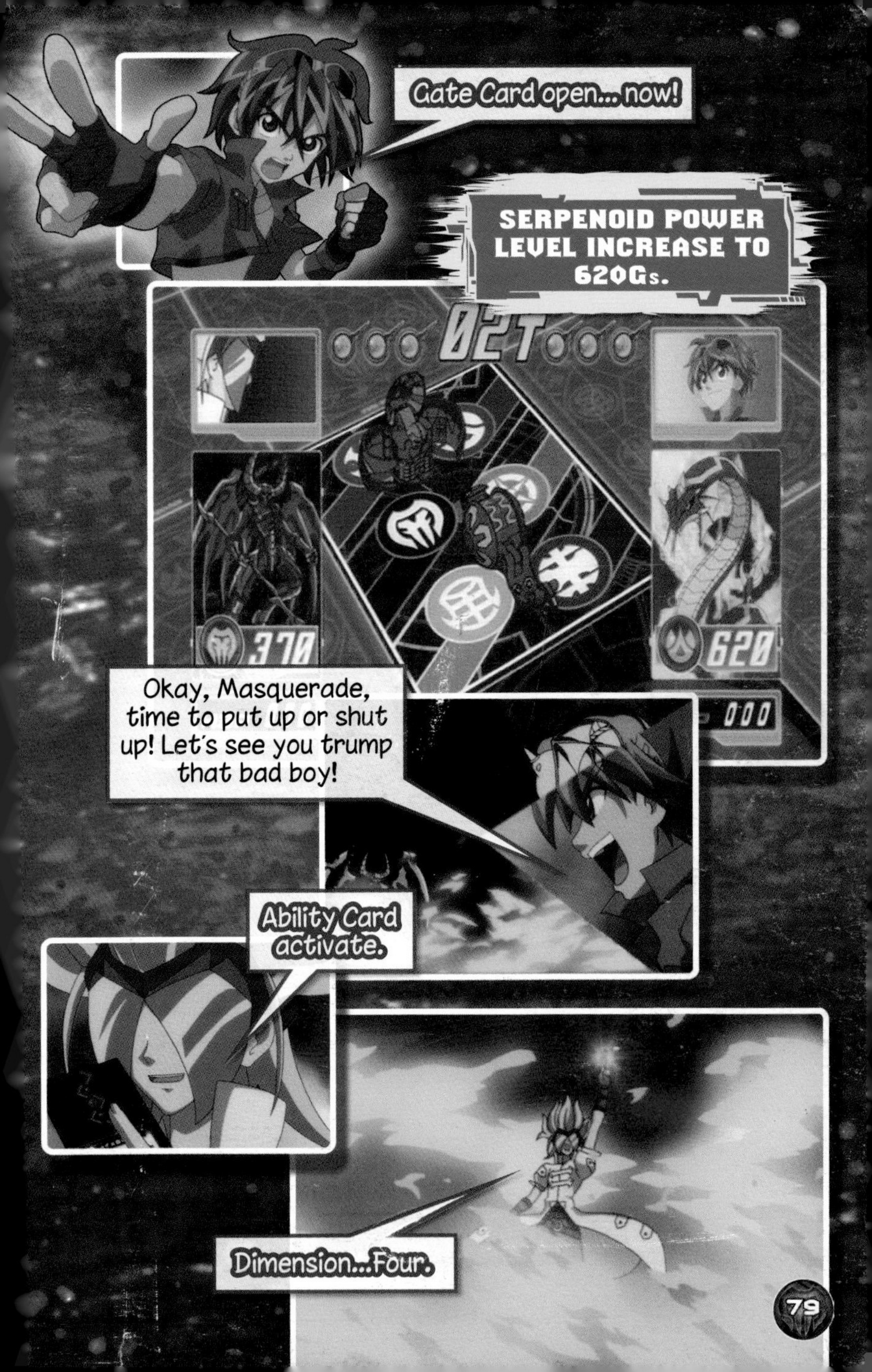

Gate Card open... now!
SERPENOID POWER LEVEL INCREASE TO 620Gs.
02T
370
620
000
Okay, Masquerade, time to put up or shut up! Let's see you trump that bad boy!
Ability Card activate.
Dimension...Four.

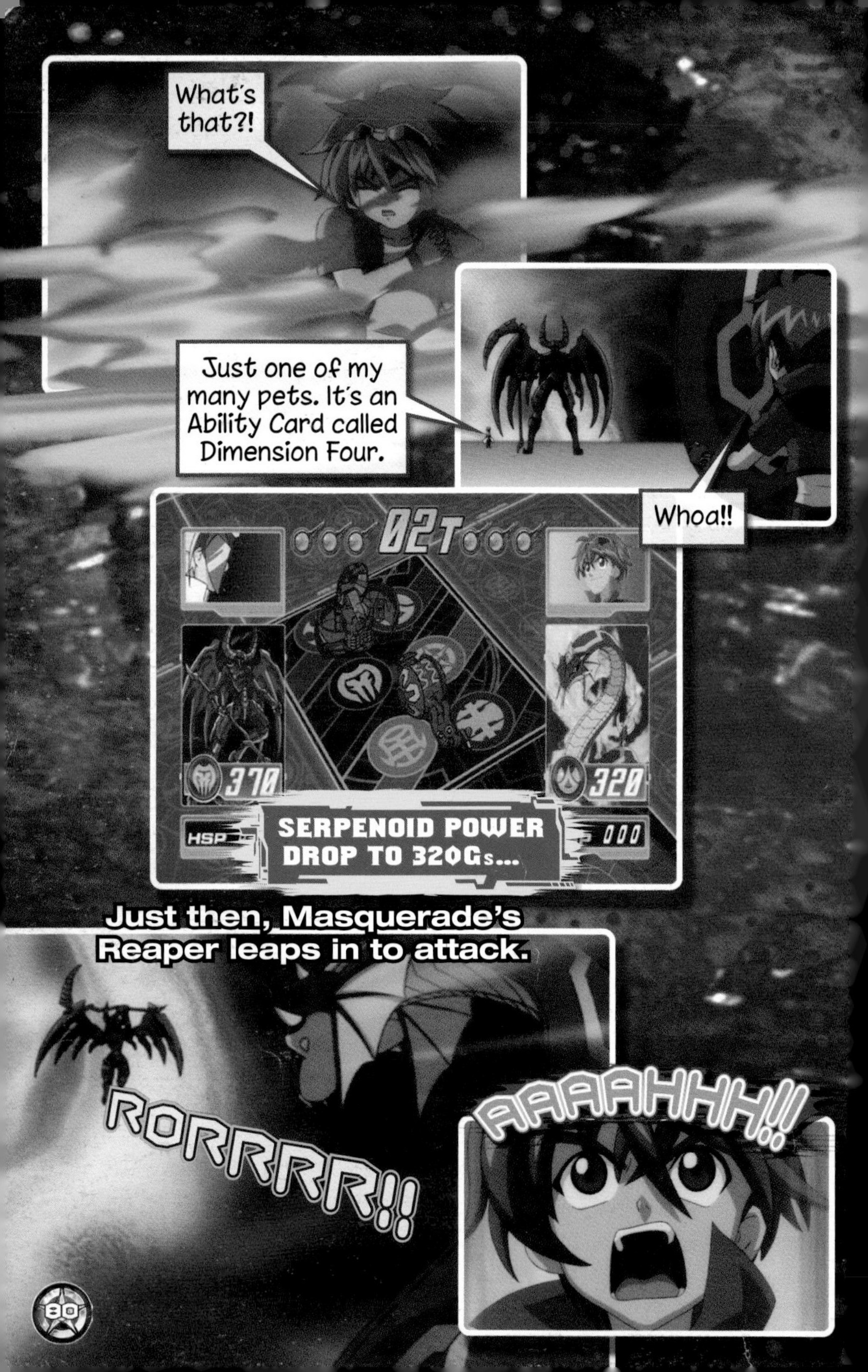
What's that?!
Just one of my many pets. It's an Ability Card called Dimension Four.
Whoa!!
02T
370
320
HSP
000
SERPENOID POWER DROP TO 320Gs...
Just then, Masquerade's Reaper leaps in to attack.
RORRRRR!!
AAAAHHH!!

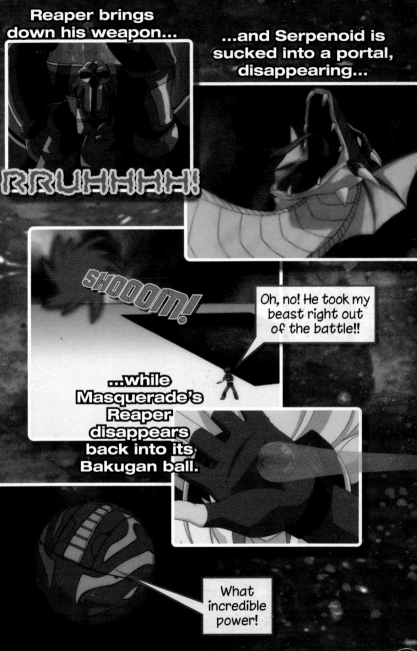

Reaper brings down his weapon...

...and Serpenoid is sucked into a portal, disappearing...

RRUHHHH!

SHOOOM!

Oh, no! He took my beast right out of the battle!!

...while Masquerade's Reaper disappears back into its Bakugan ball.

What incredible power!

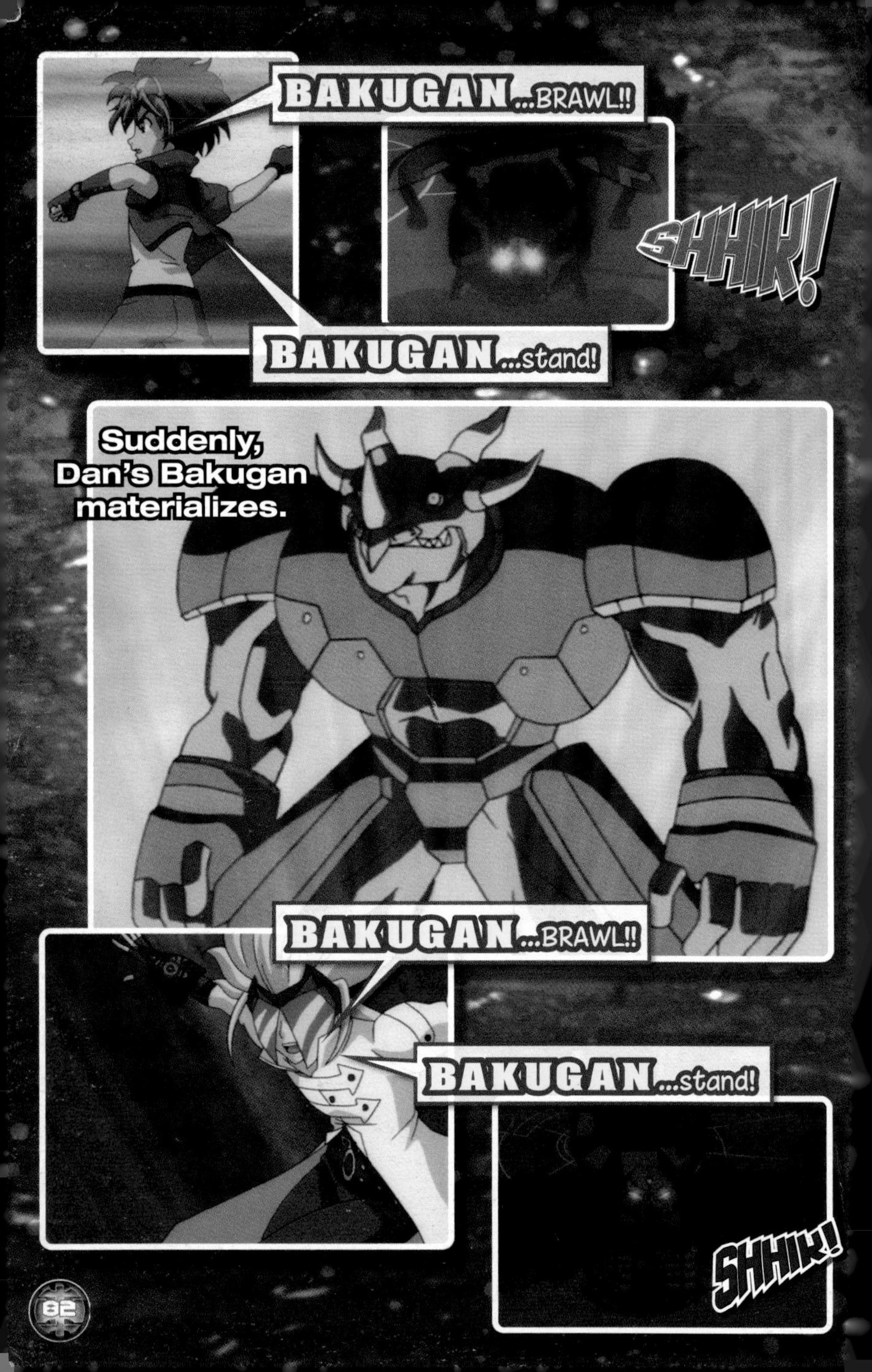
BAKUGAN...BRAWL!!
BAKUGAN...stand!
SHHIK!
Suddenly, Dan's Bakugan materializes.
BAKUGAN...BRAWL!!
BAKUGAN...stand!
SHHIK!

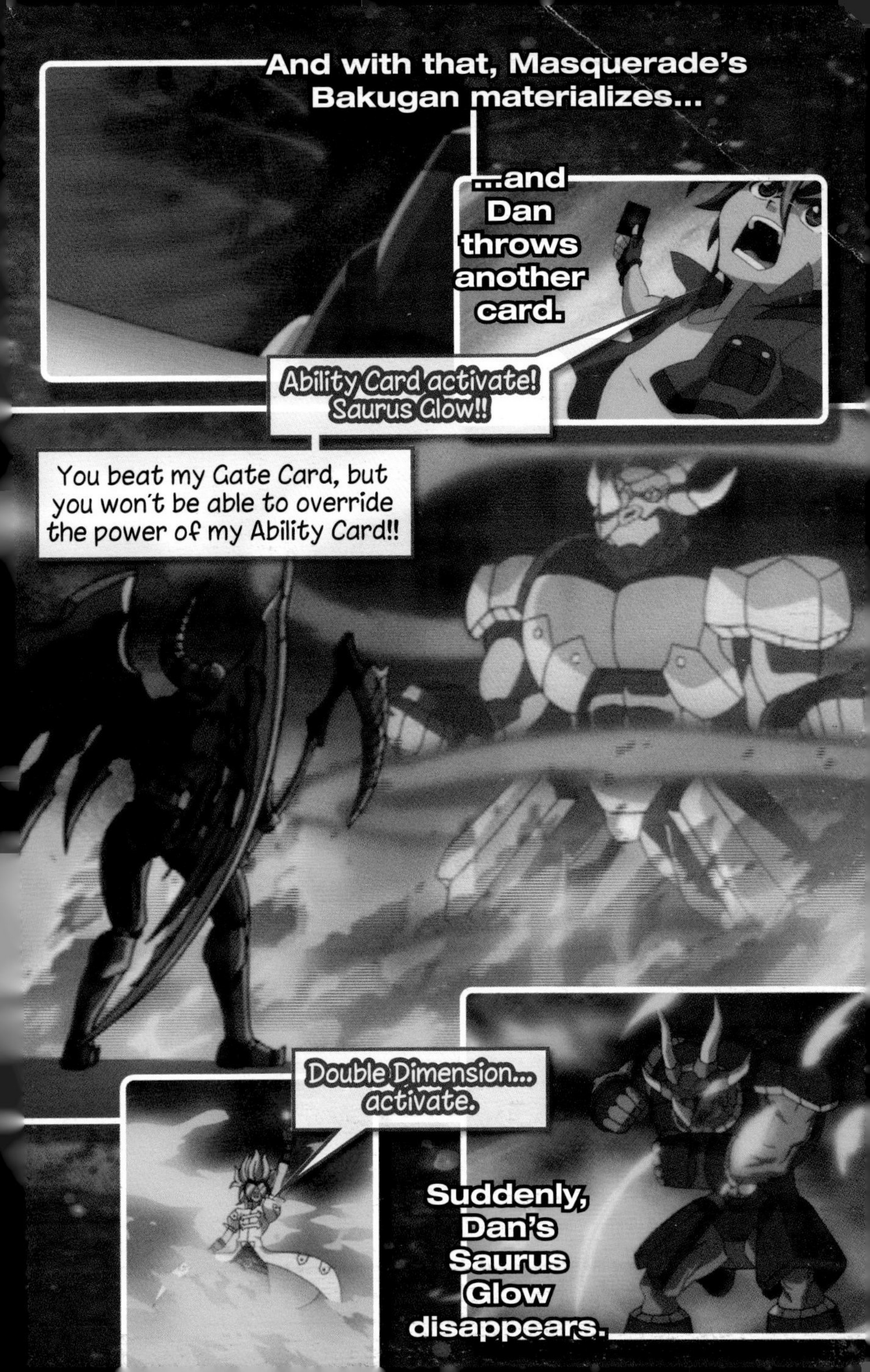
And with that, Masquerade's Bakugan materializes...
...and Dan throws another card.
Ability Card activate! Saurus Glow!!
You beat my Gate Card, but you won't be able to override the power of my Ability Card!!
Double Dimension... activate.
Suddenly, Dan's Saurus Glow disappears.

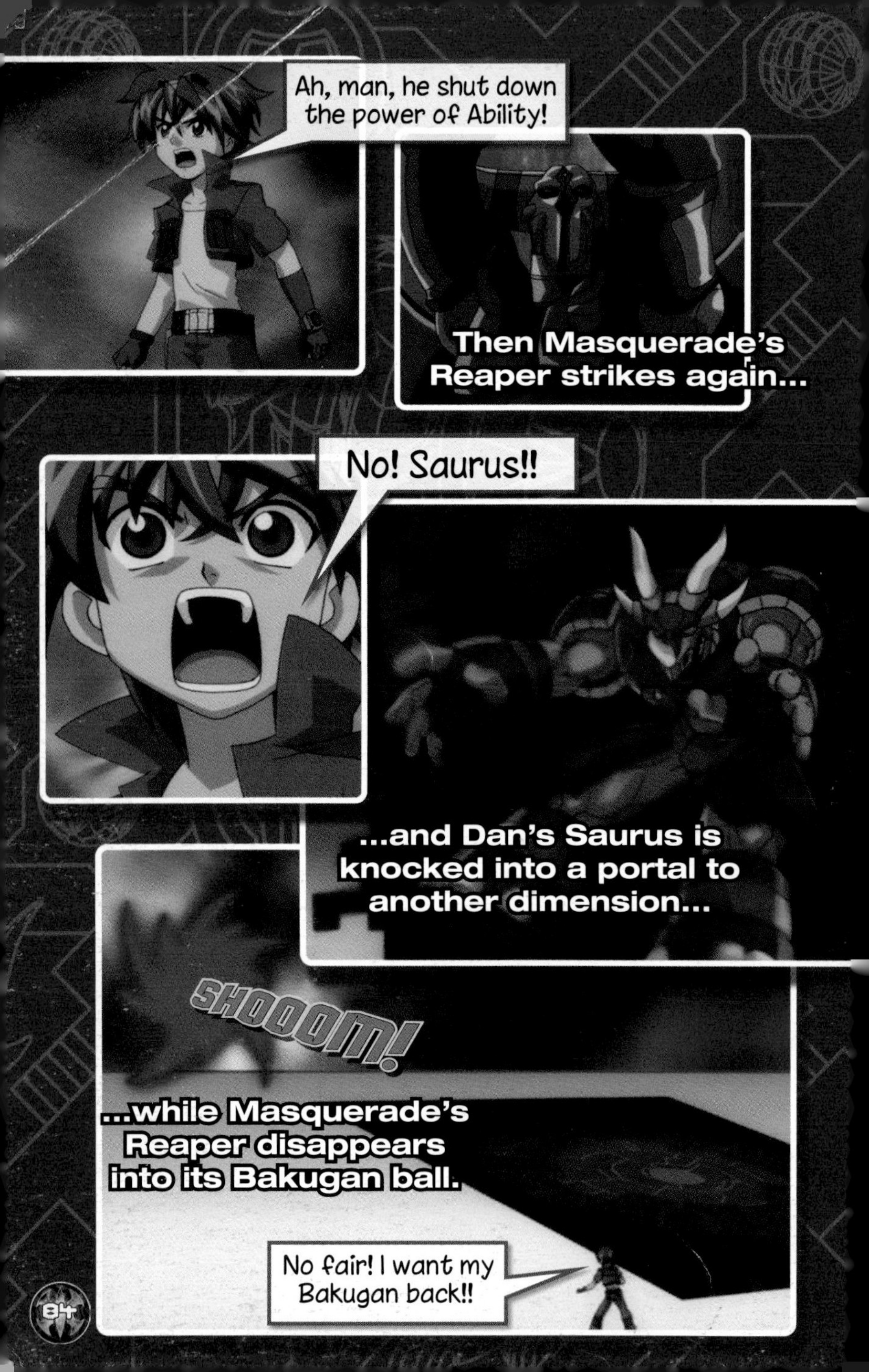
Ah, man, he shut down the power of Ability!
Then Masquerade's Reaper strikes again...
No! Saurus!!
...and Dan's Saurus is knocked into a portal to another dimension...
SHOOOM!
...while Masquerade's Reaper disappears into its Bakugan ball.
No fair! I want my Bakugan back!!

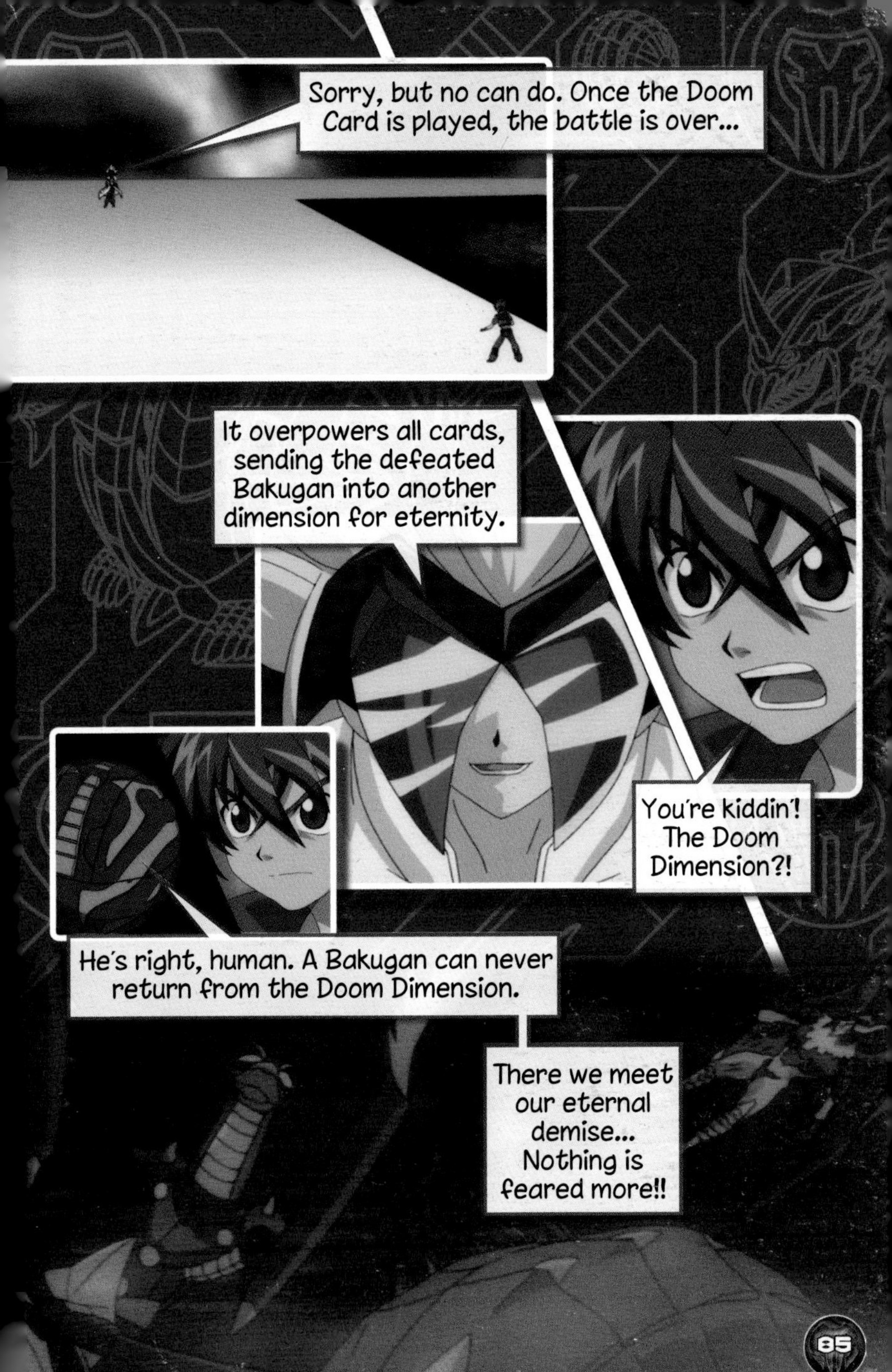
Sorry, but no can do. Once the Doom Card is played, the battle is over...
It overpowers all cards, sending the defeated Bakugan into another dimension for eternity.
You're kiddin'! The Doom Dimension?!
He's right, human. A Bakugan can never return from the Doom Dimension.
There we meet our eternal demise... Nothing is feared more!!

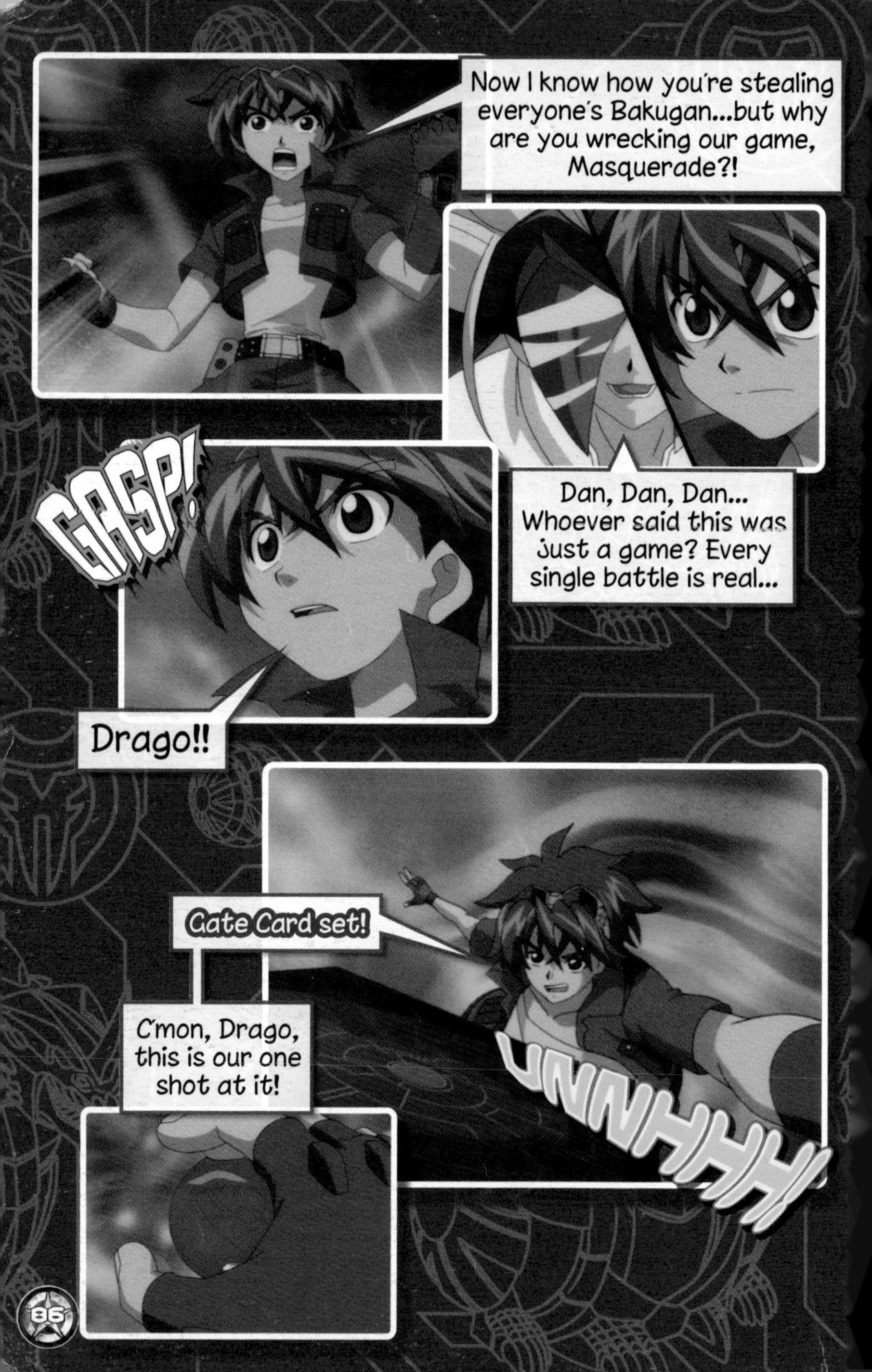
Now I know how you're stealing everyone's Bakugan...but why are you wrecking our game, Masquerade?!
Dan, Dan, Dan... Whoever said this was just a game? Every single battle is real...
GASP!
Drago!!
Gate Card set!
UNNHHH!
C'mon, Drago, this is our one shot at it!

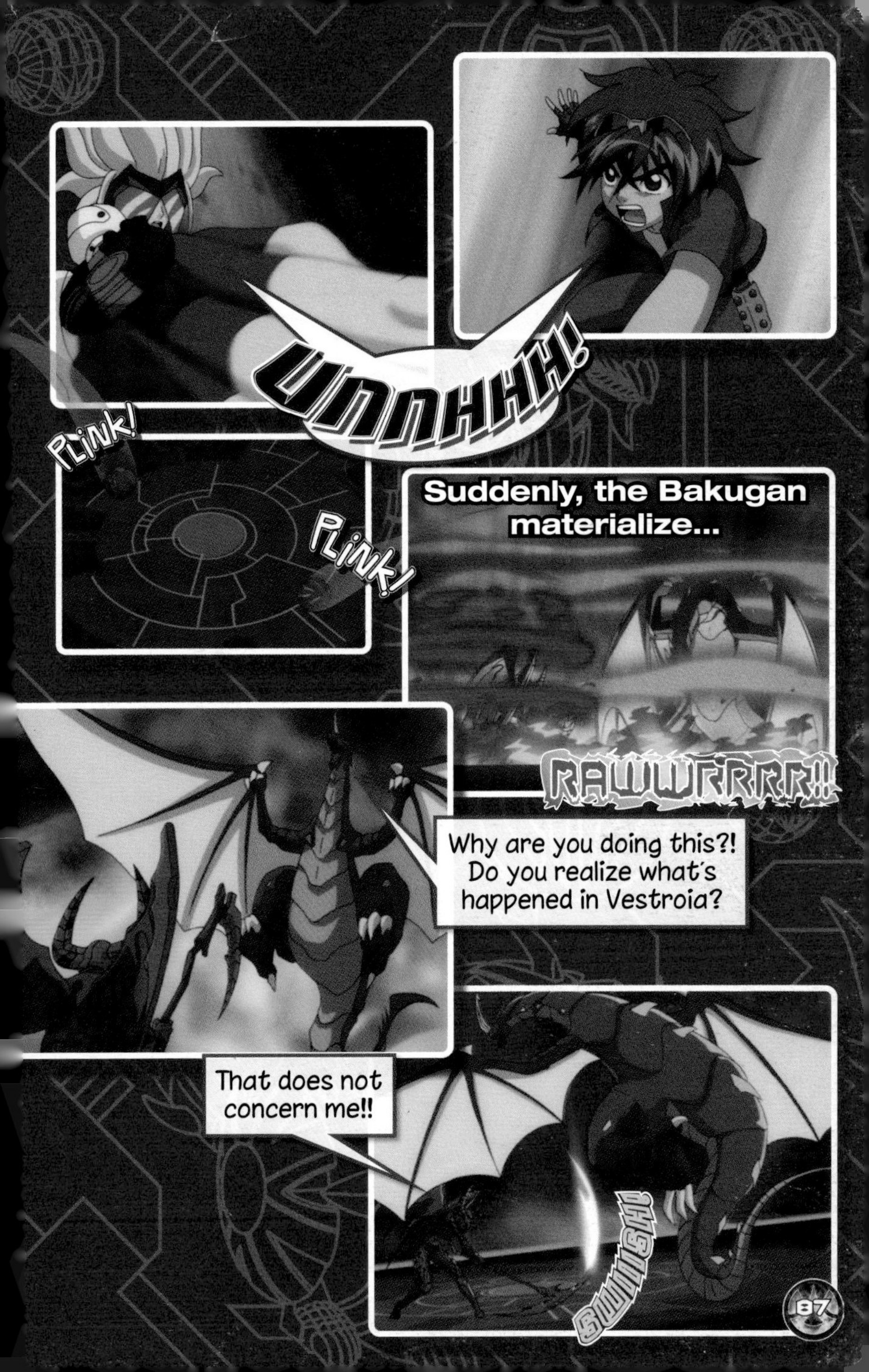
UNNHHH!
PLINK!
PLINK!
Suddenly, the Bakugan materialize...
RAWWRRRR!!
Why are you doing this?! Do you realize what's happened in Vestroia?
That does not concern me!!
BWOOSH!

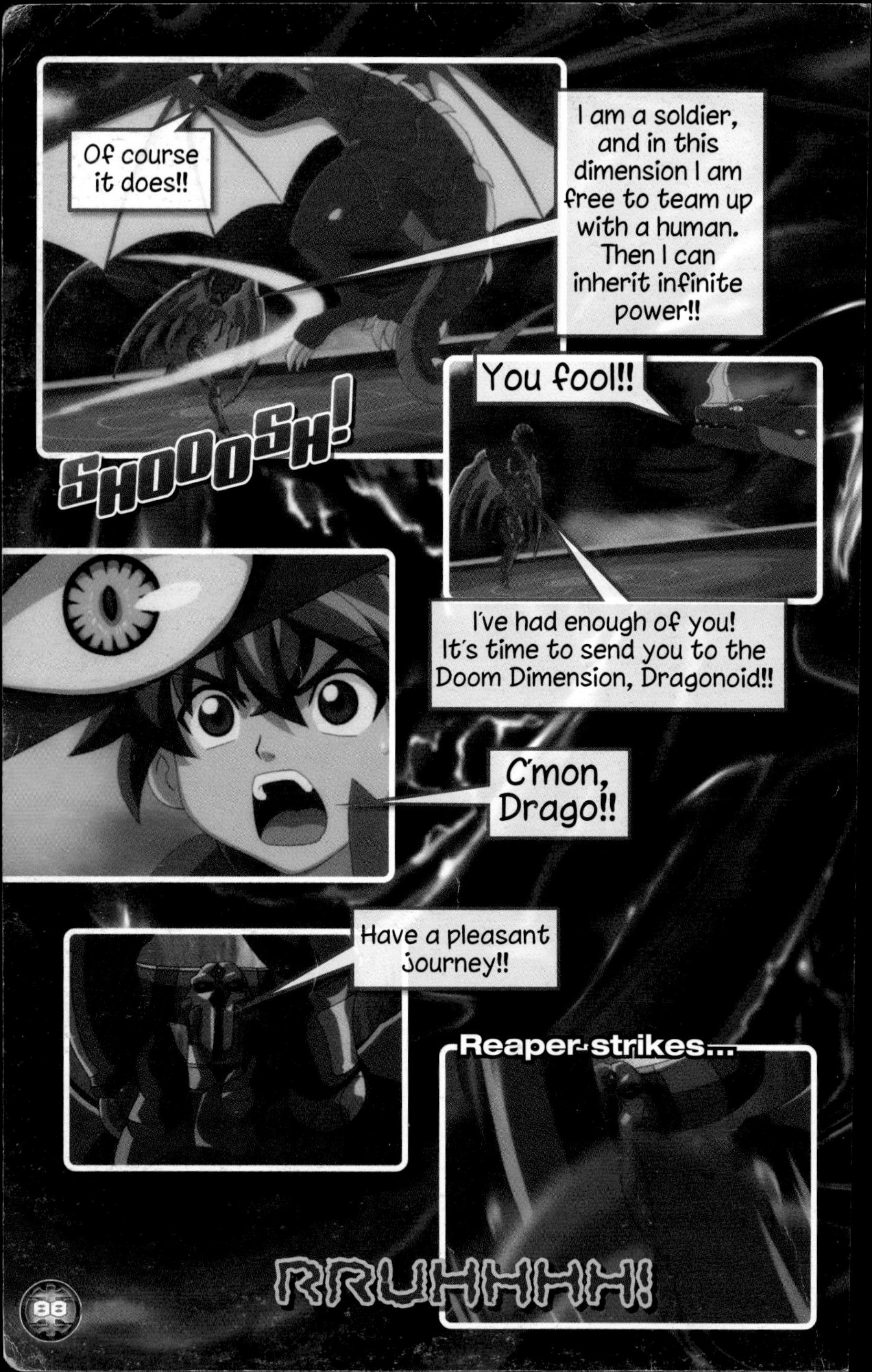

Of course it does!!
I am a soldier, and in this dimension I am free to team up with a human. Then I can inherit infinite power!!
SHOOOSH!
You fool!!
I've had enough of you! It's time to send you to the Doom Dimension, Dragonoid!!
C'mon, Drago!!
Have a pleasant journey!!
Reaper strikes...
RRUHHHH!

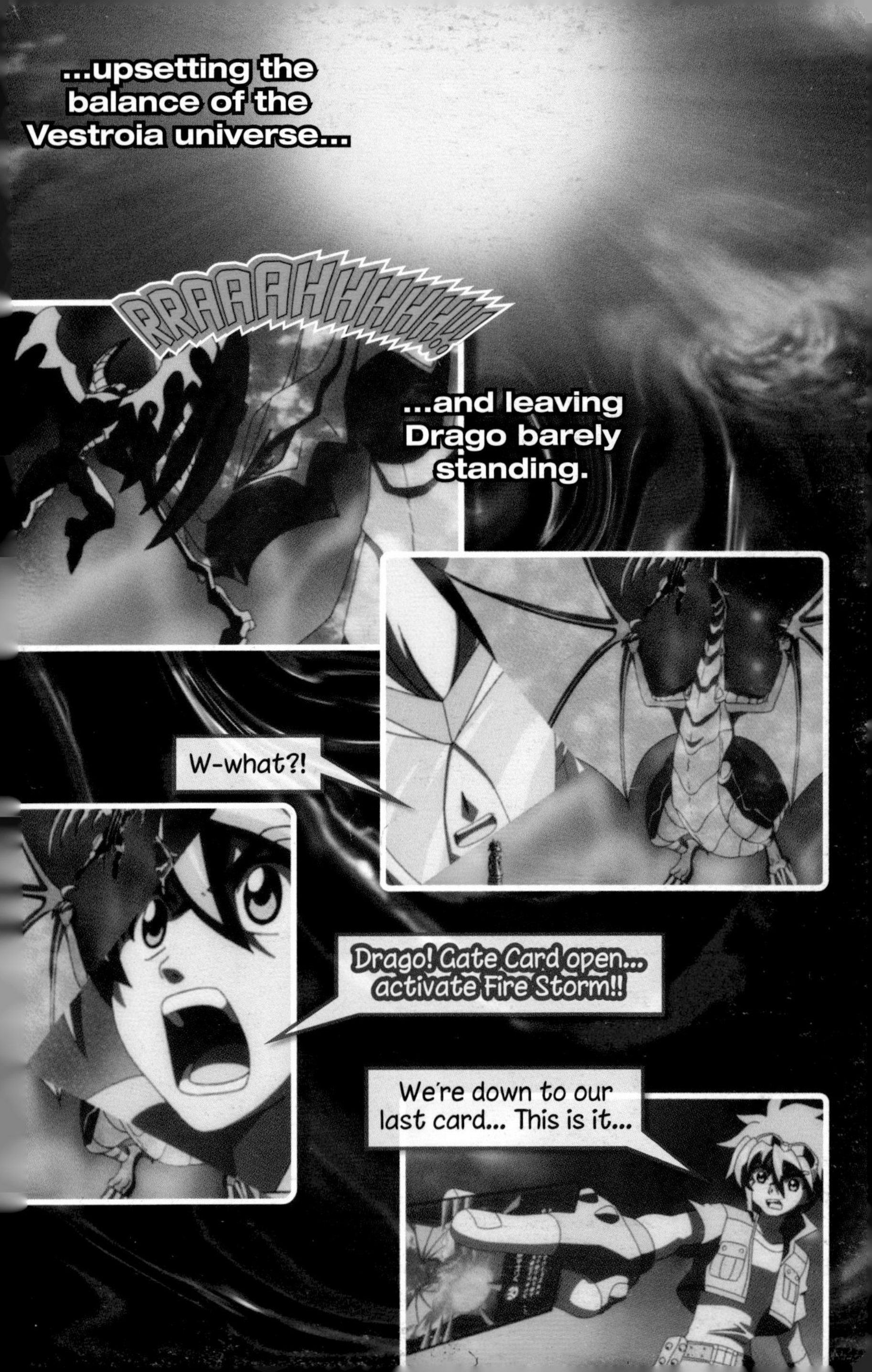
...upsetting the balance of the Vestroia universe...
RRAAAHHHHH!!
...and leaving Drago barely standing.
W-what?!
Drago! Gate Card open... activate Fire Storm!!
We're down to our last card... This is it...

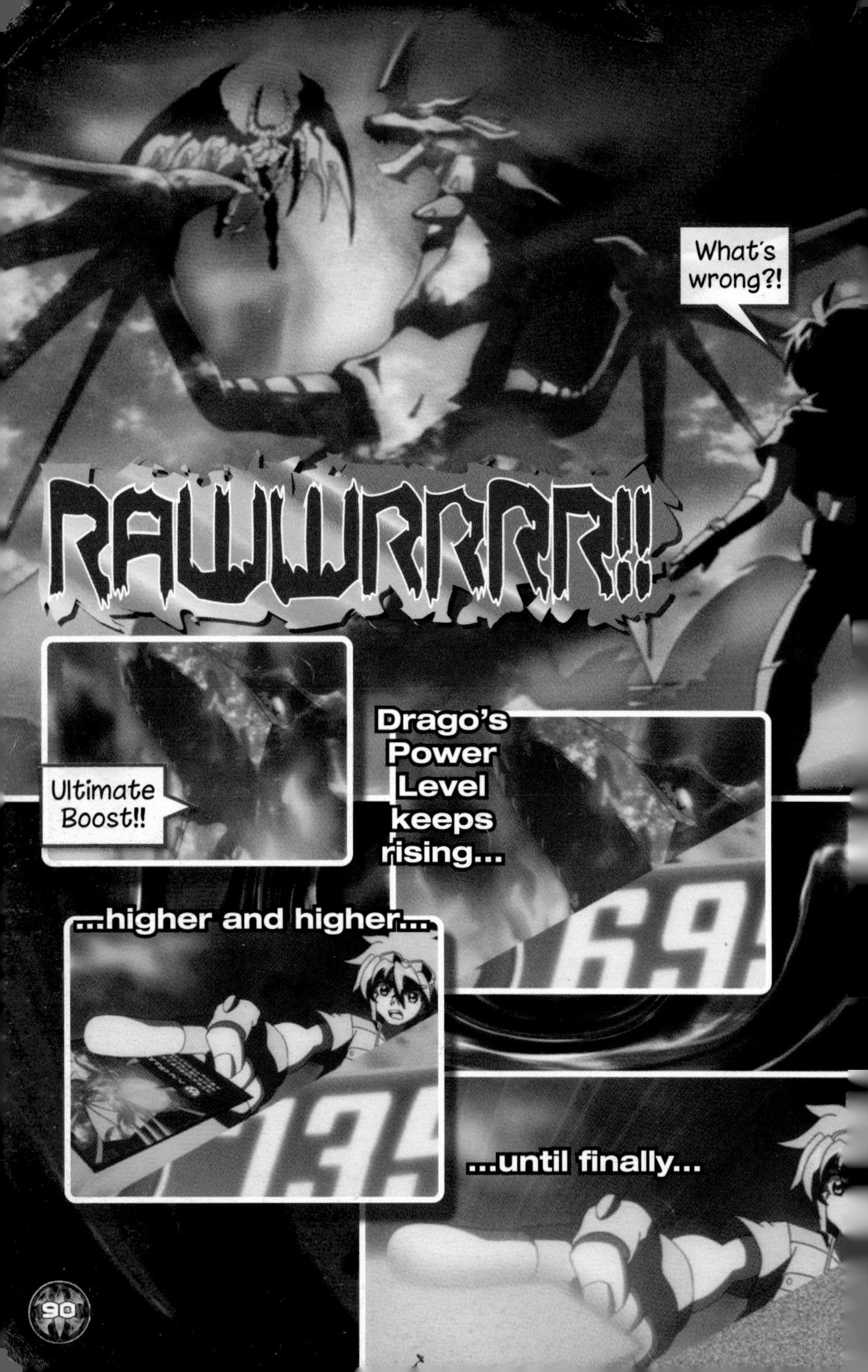
What's wrong?!
RAWWRRRR!!
Ultimate Boost!!
Drago's Power Level keeps rising...
...higher and higher...
...until finally...

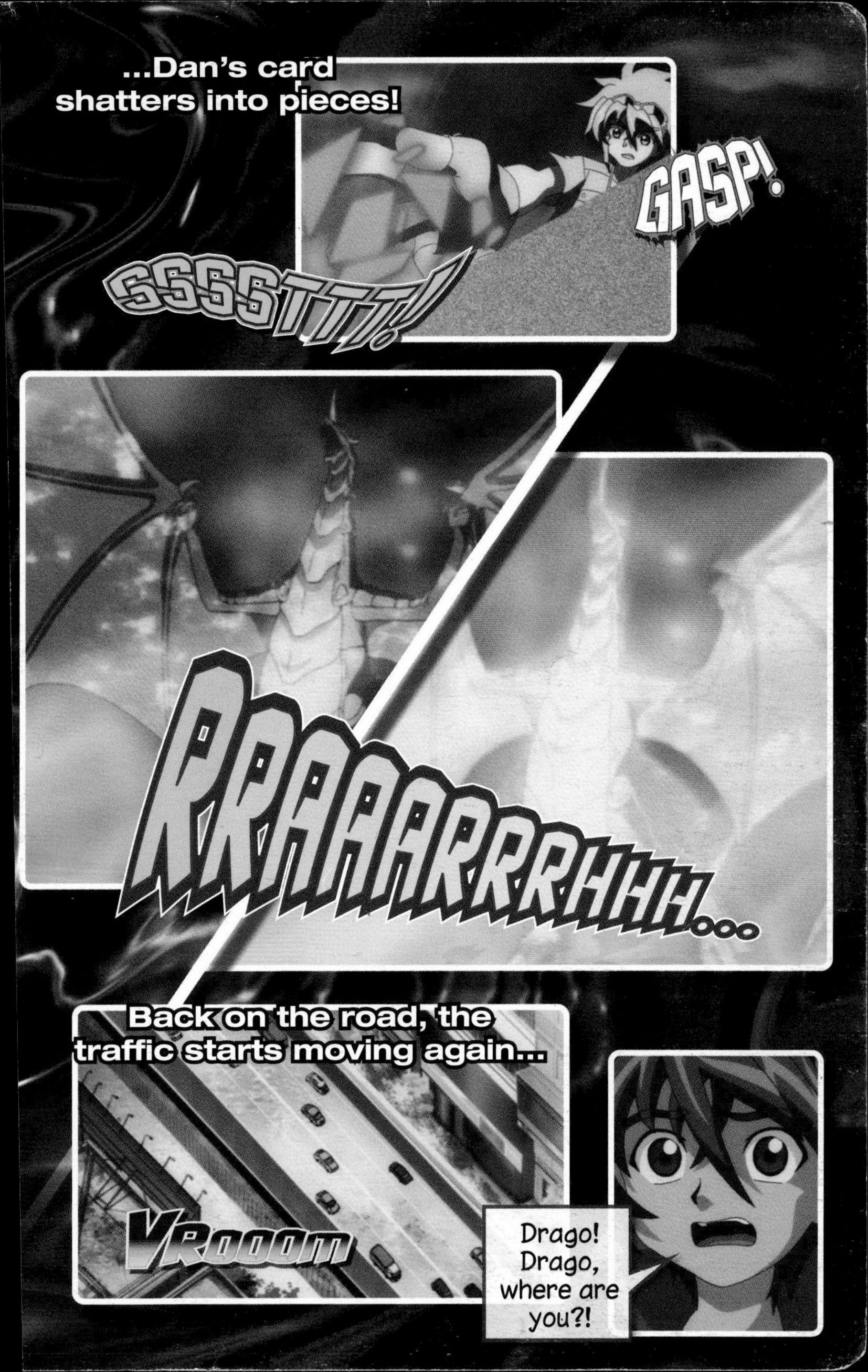
...Dan's card shatters into pieces!
GASP!
SSSSTTTT!
RRAAAARRRHHH...
Back on the road, the traffic starts moving again...
VROOOM
Drago! Drago, where are you?!

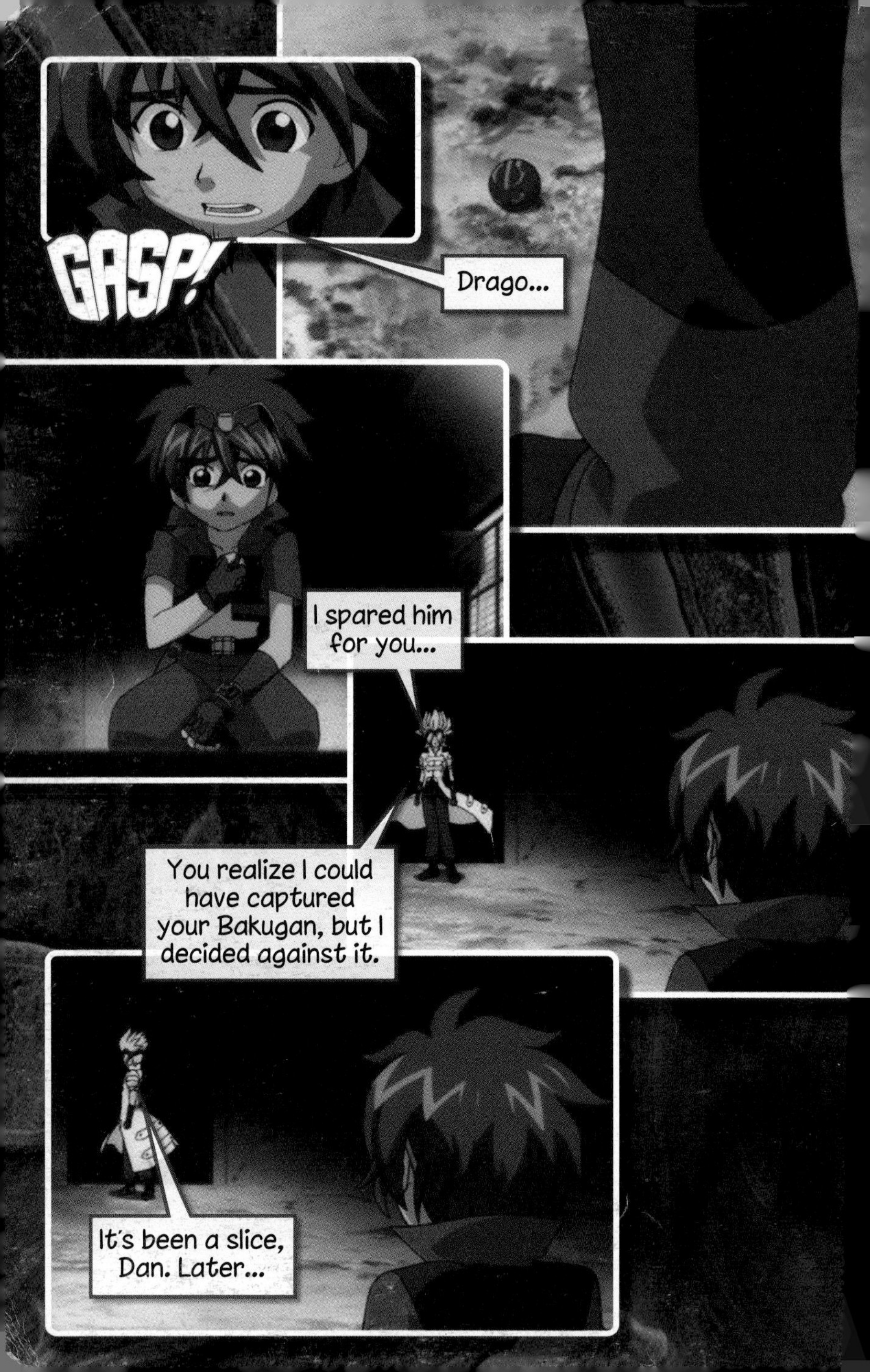
GASP!
Drago...
I spared him for you...
You realize I could have captured your Bakugan, but I decided against it.
It's been a slice, Dan. Later...

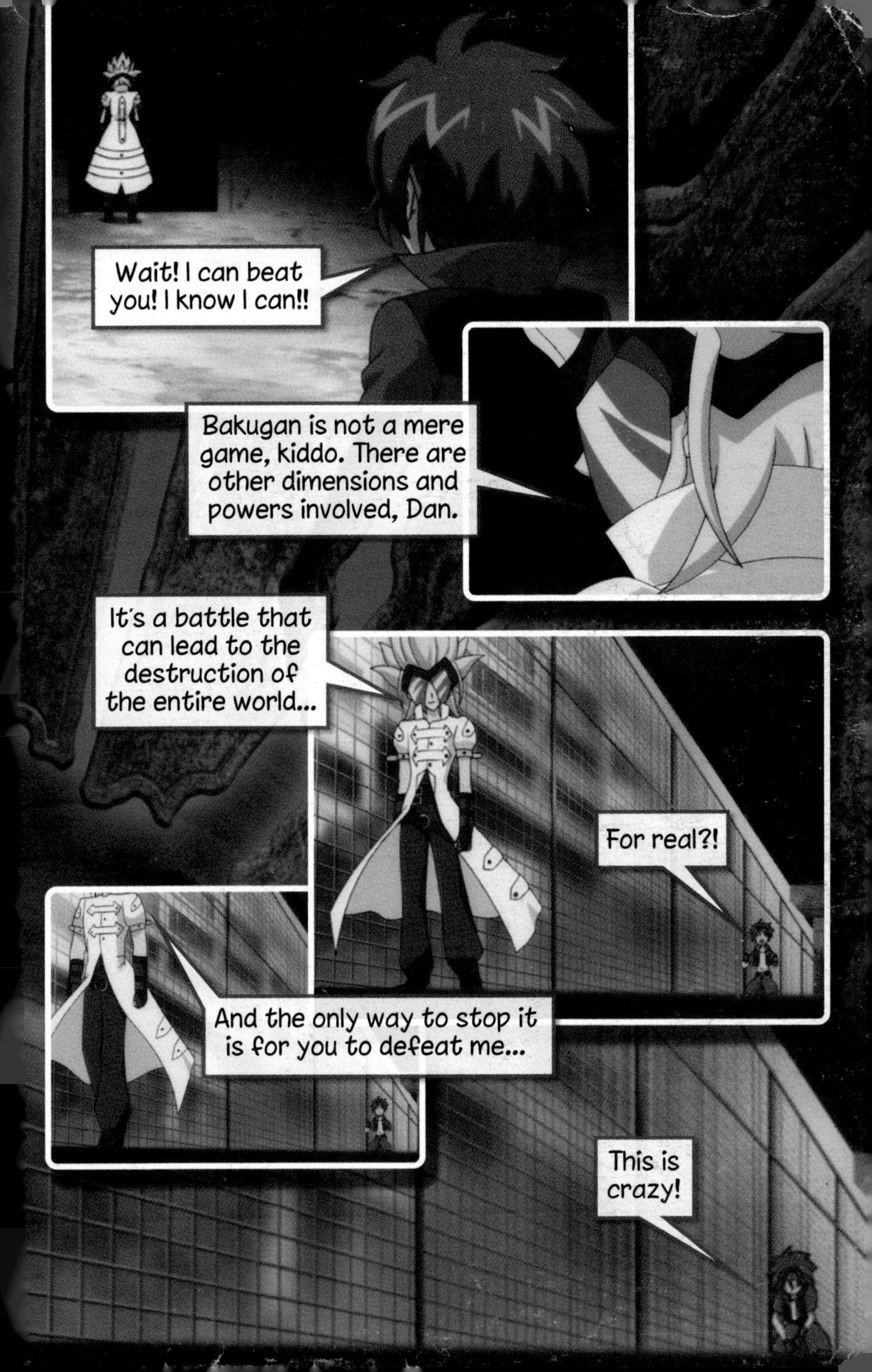
Wait! I can beat you! I know I can!!
Bakugan is not a mere game, kiddo. There are other dimensions and powers involved, Dan.
It's a battle that can lead to the destruction of the entire world...
For real?!
And the only way to stop it is for you to defeat me...
This is crazy!

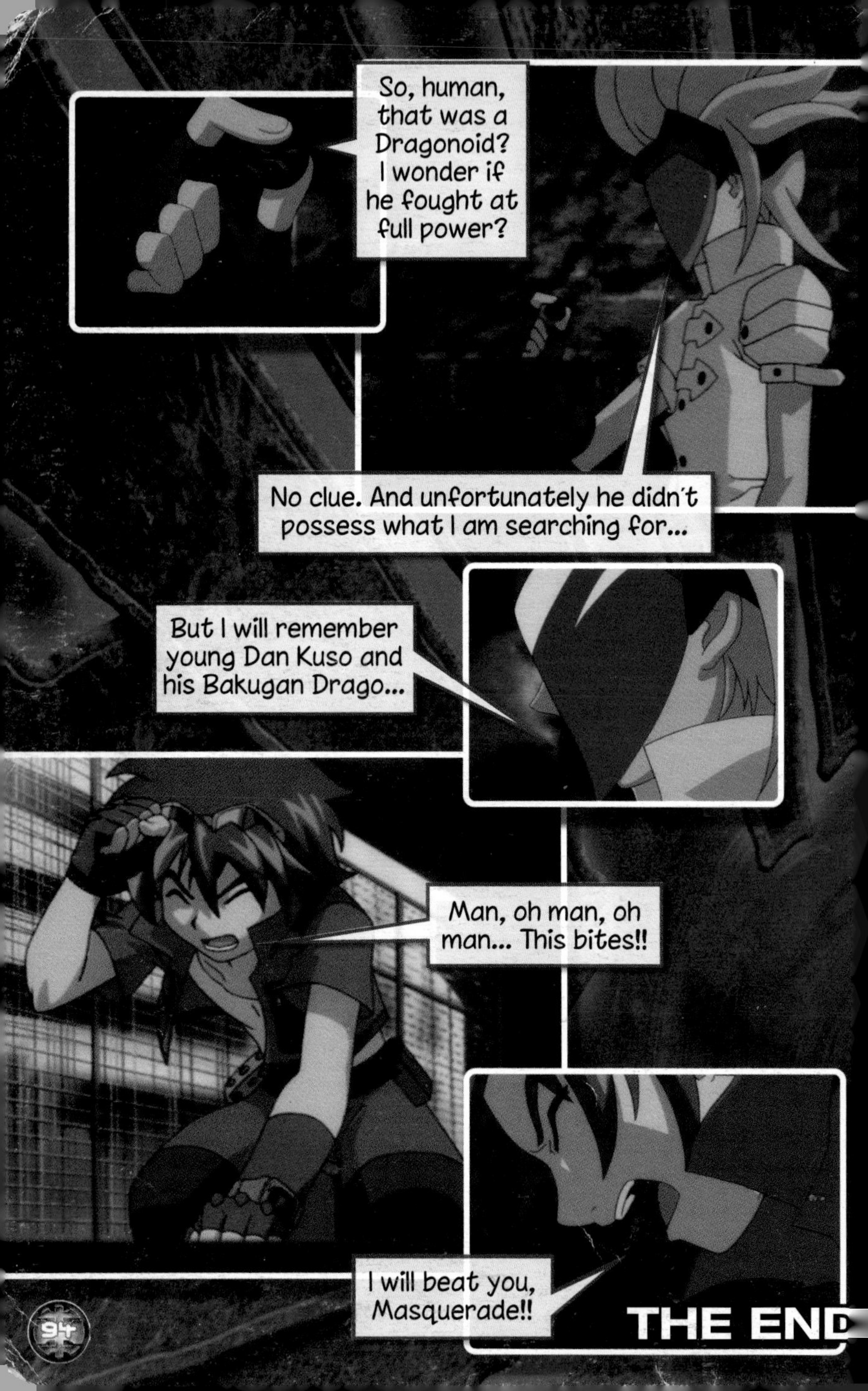
So, human, that was a Dragonoid? I wonder if he fought at full power?
No clue. And unfortunately he didn't possess what I am searching for...
But I will remember young Dan Kuso and his Bakugan Drago...
Man, oh man, oh man... This bites!!
I will beat you, Masquerade!!
THE END

PREVIEW OF VOLUME 3:
A FEUD BETWEEN FRIENDS

BAKUGAN
BATTLE BRAWLERS

"In the next volume..."

SHHIK!

"...Drago and I make a little noise."

GASP!

RRRRARRR!

"Oh sure, my parents are a little worried..."

"...but I told 'em not to worry..."

"...we wouldn't burn the house down."

RAWWRRRR!!

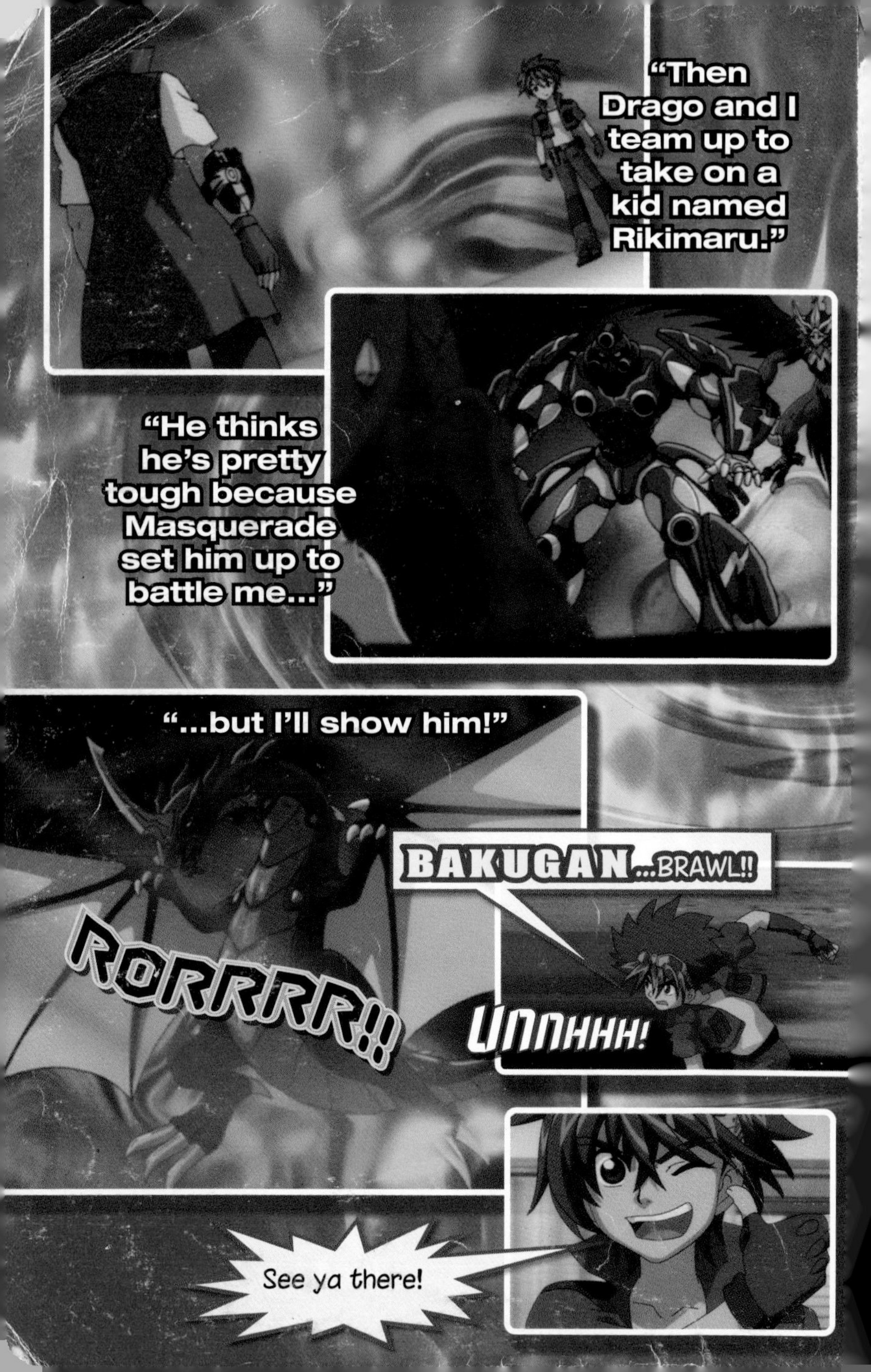
"Then Drago and I team up to take on a kid named Rikimaru."
"He thinks he's pretty tough because Masquerade set him up to battle me..."
"...but I'll show him!"
RORRRRR!!
BAKUGAN ...BRAWL!!
UNNHHH!
See ya there!